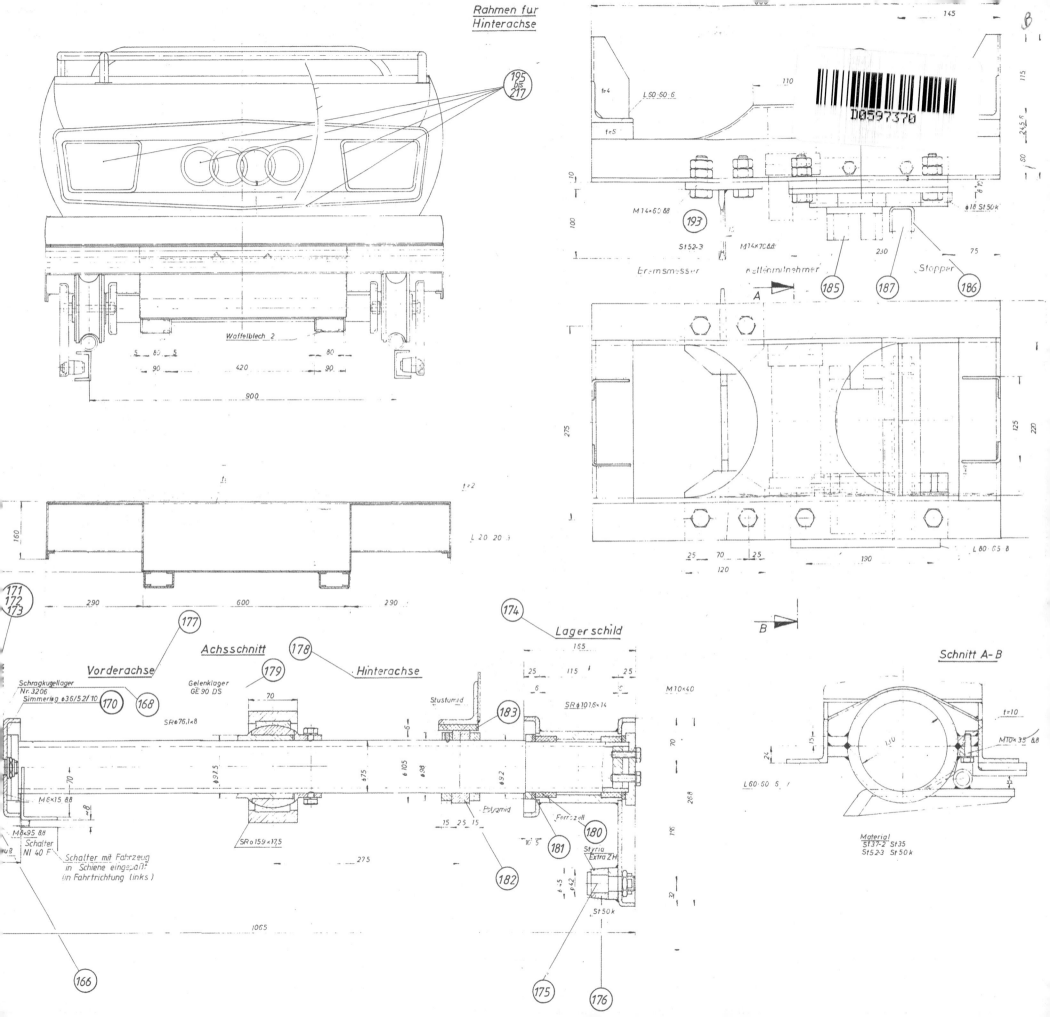

Rahmen für
Hinterachse

Waffelblech 2

Vorderachse

Achsschnitt

Hinterachse

Lager schild

Schnitt A-B

Bremsmesser

Kettenmitnehmer

Stopper

Schalter mit Fahrzeug
in Schiene eingepaßt
(in Fahrtrichtung links)

Schragkugellager
Nr. 3206
Simmering ⌀36/52/10

Gelenklager
GE 90 DS

Material
St 37-2 St 35
St 52-3 St 50k

D0597370

Roller Coasters

A Thrill Seeker's Guide to the Ultimate Scream Machines

Roller Coasters

A Thrill Seeker's Guide to the Ultimate Scream Machines

ROBERT COKER

BARNES
& NOBLE

NEW YORK

2006 Barnes & Noble

ISBN-13: 978-0-7607-7615-5
ISBN-10: 0-7607-7615-6

The Library of Congress has catalogued earlier editions under the
Library of Congress Control Number: 2003101103

Printed and bound in China

3   5   7   9   10   8   6   4   2

Title Page: An archetypical example of Arrow's corkscrew coasters is the *Python,* which opened in 1976 at Busch Gardens Tampa. It was considered remarkable at the time, but is now practically a kiddie coaster compared to this park's newer major attractions, like the dueling *Gwazi* woodies and its two steel Bolliger & Mabillard coasters, *Kumba* and *Montu.*

Opposite: One of the more unusual coaster installations is the Arrow Dynamics–designed *Canyon Blaster,* a multiloop ride that operates inside the Adventuredome at Circus Circus in Las Vegas, Nevada. This coaster features two vertical loops, a double-flipping corkscrew, and some narrow scrapes around and through the Adventuredome's artificial mountain.

Dedication

For my mom, Katherine, and for New York City, birthplace
of the modern roller coaster and the greatest city in the world

Acknowledgments

First and foremost, I must acknowledge a few existing books that were invaluable resources in preparing some of what you're about to read. Robert Cartmell's *The Incredible Scream Machine* remains the definitive work on the history of roller coasters, and I highly recommend it for anyone who wishes to learn in much greater detail how the modern roller coaster came to be. Also of assistance were Steven J. Urbanowicz's *The Roller Coaster Lover's Companion* and Todd H. Throgmorton's *Roller Coasters of America* for their comprehensive statistics, dates, names, places, and the like.

I'd also like to tip my hat to everyone who works at the parks for making my life so much richer. Ditto for those who actually design and build thrill rides. Where we'd be without these wonderful people, I'd rather not imagine.

Last, I must thank my mom, for the countless hours she so patiently waited by the exits, and for her endless love and support.

Contents

Introduction

I Scream Therefore I Am 8

Chapter 1

Laying Down the Tracks—Roller Coaster History 12

Chapter 2

Everybody Loves a Woodie—Wooden Coaster Rides 24

Chapter 3

Hot Wheels on Steel Coasters 50

Chapter 4

Extreme Machines 90

Chapter 5

Rocket Coasters 132

Chapter 6

Aftershock 140

Appendix 154

Glossary 157

Index 158

These are the days of miracle and wonder, friends. It wasn't so long ago that a 100-foot (30.5m) roller coaster was considered gargantuan; many now stand more than twice as high, and a pair of the world's tallest are more than *four times* that size. Roller coasters are now bigger, faster, and more death-defying than ever before. And, at long last, in 1997 we were blessed with *Superman: The Escape*, the first 100-mile-per-hour (161kph) attraction. Astounding.

The headlong pace at which scream machines are evolving begs the question: why do we ride them? Every coaster fanatic has been on the receiving end of this query more than once in his or her life; I know I sure hear it a lot. I'm always tempted to answer, "Well, duh, because it's fun." But that's not an evenhanded reply. Of course *we* think roller coasters are fun; the folks usually posing the question are of a different mind altogether.

How, then, do we respond? There must be a good answer because thrill rides are as popular as ever. The International Association of Amusement Parks and Attractions (IAAPA) estimates that attendance at U.S. parks in 2000 hit an all-time high of around 317 million. What's the primary draw for those hundreds of millions of ravenous thrill seekers? That's right—big rides. And the parks cater to our needs, in many cases sparing no expense. Tremendous roller coasters boast price tags in the tens of millions of dollars; the tallest, longest, and fastest continuous-circuit coaster, Japan's *Steel Dragon 2000*, ran up a tab of more than $51 million. The whopping expenditures are money well spent when you consider how attendance rates can jump by significant percentages when an amusement park debuts a new, record-breaking attraction.

Getting back to the issue at hand, our answer to the "Why" question must acknowledge this fact: we like being scared. Why do we like being scared? As Eleanor Roosevelt aptly put it, "You gain strength, courage, and confidence by every experience in which you really stop to look fear in the face. You are able to say to yourself, 'I have lived through this horror. I can take the next thing that comes along.' You must do the thing you think you cannot do."

And unlike, say, cliff diving or alligator wrestling, thrill rides allow us to face our fears in a controlled, secure way. Contrary to what many lurid tabloid-television specials would have us believe, modern scream machines are unquestionably safe. According to figures supplied by the IAAPA, the odds of sustaining an injury that would require hospitalization while visiting a fixed-site amusement park are about 1 in 23 million and the odds of a fatality are about 1 in 500 million. Based on the U.S. Consumer Products Safety Commission's estimates, more people were injured in 1999 using bicycles (614,594), trampolines (98,889), and golf equipment (47,386) than while on amusement park rides (7,260, only 138 of which required hospitalization). And the majority of thrill-ride injuries are usually the result of passenger tomfoolery, not equipment malfunction.

Our biological reactions to thrill ride–induced terror also help to explain why we crave it so. Scientists do not yet have a comprehensive understanding of the entire process, but key mechanisms in the brain's complex fear-response system have

Left: A maintenance worker walks the tracks of Coney Island's long-gone *Tornado* (originally the *Bobs*, 1926), greasing up the chain lift in preparation for the start of another summer season. And one year after the modern roller coaster's birth at Coney Island in 1884, Philip Hinckle is credited with adding a hoist to the mechanical cable system on the coaster he built at Coney Island, spurring the creation of the chain lift that is still in use today.

Pages 10–11: Riders become a blur as they speed along on *Jetline* at Gröna Lund Amusement Park in Stockholm, Sweden. This Schwarzkopf/Zierer-designed coaster, a non-looping steel twister, shares the same layout as *BMRX* at Japan's Kobe Portopialand.

been identified. In 1999, I spoke with Dr. Bruce Kapp, a professor of psychology at the University of Vermont and a leading researcher in the study of fear and its effects on the mind and body. Dr. Kapp described what he and other researchers are discovering.

The process begins inside a part of the brain called the amygdala. "This is where the brain endows experience with an emotional tone, where we are conditioned to fear specific stimuli," Kapp explained. In experiments, Kapp has been able to illustrate the amygdala's role by studying rats and their "species-typical" fear response. First, he places a normal, healthy rodent inside a box with a sedated cat. The rat will stay motionless, urinate, and defecate, all signs that the poor critter is terrified of its feline adversary. Kapp then surgically removes the rat's amygdala and puts the rat back in a box with another tranquilized kitty. This time, instead of cowering in a corner, the rat walks right up to and crawls all over the cat. Without the amygdala to tell the rest of the brain to be alarmed, the rat is literally fearless.

So how does the amygdala communicate with the rest of our gray matter? Huge networks of nerve fibers hot-wire this all-important tissue to various neural regions that control our cardioregulatory systems, command the release of certain chemicals, and process our sensory input. At that delicious moment when we teeter over the brink of a huge coaster hill, the amygdala instantly transmits its distress signals far and wide, "jacking up" our brain. Adrenaline floodgates open. Our heart pounds, our blood pressure soars, and our breathing becomes rapid. External senses are put on full alert. In microseconds, we are jolted into a heightened state of awareness.

This condition may not be everybody's cup of tea, but for true thrill seekers, that feeling of amplified arousal is just what we're after. For a few brief minutes, we feel more "alive." Further, at the amygdala's request, pain-suppressing endorphins are released, a potentially lifesaving reaction when faced with real

danger. If we're under attack, we need to fight or flee, and in either case, we can't stop to nurse our wounds; hence, we become self-drugged so that we feel minimal discomfort. Endorphins, as marathoners well know, are responsible for what is commonly called a runner's high. Our fear can actually generate a mildly euphoric buzz.

I'm guessing this may also explain why thrill rides are continually growing in size and intensity. As we become inured to the horror generated by a 150-foot (46m) free fall, we need something even taller to get our nervous system operating at DefCon 1 status. We are addicted to this high, and we need ever more potent doses of horror to reach the exalted plane.

Finally, there's no denying the appeal of a situation that allows us to scream ourselves silly without regard to decorum. Got problems at work? Try letting loose with a good shriek around the watercooler and see how long it takes before security "escorts" you out the back door. For many, roller coasters are a release valve on the pressure cooker of life. After a solid day of romping through an amusement park, I am dazed, exhausted, and utterly at peace with the world.

True thrill seekers are not limited by age, sex, class, profession, or race; we come in every shape and size imaginable. I've seen preteens board attractions I wouldn't have dared approach when I was their age, and I've met grandparents and great-grandparents who don't think twice about heading right for the tallest coaster they can find. Doctors, lawyers, ministers, teachers, actors, athletes—you can find a thrill-ride junkie no matter where you look.

Some folks will always think we're certifiably loony, but this quote, attributed to one Angela Monet, lays it right on the line: "Those who danced were thought to be quite insane by those who could not hear the music." *We* can hear the music, loud and clear.

Ready to dance?

LAYING DOWN THE TRACKS—ROLLER COASTER HISTORY

CHAPTER 1

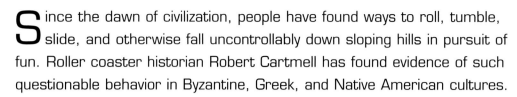

Since the dawn of civilization, people have found ways to roll, tumble, slide, and otherwise fall uncontrollably down sloping hills in pursuit of fun. Roller coaster historian Robert Cartmell has found evidence of such questionable behavior in Byzantine, Greek, and Native American cultures.

But the first attempt to create something closely related to today's rail-riding wonders can be found in Russia many centuries ago....

Russian Ice Slides

Dateline: fifteenth century, downtown Saint Petersburg.

It's another brutal Russian winter, and as always folks are looking to have some fun. Huddled around a fire, two good citizens stare out at the frostbitten landscape.

"So, Pyotr, looks like we'll be getting more snow today."

"Yes, Yuri. As they say, what else is new?"

"My friend, we need some new ideas for what we can do to pass the time—a new diversion, perhaps something that will make us scream with giddy pleasure."

"Yes, screaming would take our minds off this wretched cold."

There is a stillness to the air as Pyotr and Yuri ponder this question. Suddenly, Pyotr leaps to his feet and bellows, "Hey, Yuri, why don't we build a wooden ramp, allow water to freeze on this ramp, fashion some sort of sled, and slide down this ramp at high velocity?!"

And so was born the first Russian Ice Slide. Sure, it was a crude idea, potentially dangerous even, but it was a stroke of genius and it caught on quickly. Ice Slides, some as tall as 70 feet (21.5m), began popping up in villages throughout Russia. Passengers would climb a staircase to a large platform at the top of the long, sloping ramp. There, they would board a "sled," nothing more than a huge block of ice. A cockpit of sorts was chiseled out of the block and lined with straw—sounds comfy, doesn't it? As I'm sure you've guessed, there wasn't much of a lap bar. A rope tied around a hole in the ice was the only means of keeping riders fastened to their careening cube. The initial drop was very steep, but gradually the ramp leveled off and the base of the slide was sometimes sprinkled with sand to ensure that riders eventually came to a halt. Daily watering maintained the icy surface of the ramp, and regular riders became adept at piloting their frozen projectiles.

Once the local royalty got wind of this development, they took to it as well, but riding big frosty slabs was out of the question. True sleds were

Right: The *Promenades Aeriennes* of Beaujon Gardens in Paris, France, was one of the first successful translations of Russia's Ice Slides into something resembling a modern roller coaster. At first, ride operators had to push vehicles up to the top of the structure, but by 1826, a cable mechanism was added to tow the cars up the incline, foreshadowing the development of the modern chain lift system. And with its side-by-side, mirrored courses, the *Promenades Aeriennes* also introduced the concept of a racing coaster.

fashioned for the royal hindquarters, eventually becoming ornate, sumptuously decorated conveyances. And as Ice Slides became the major attractions at winter festivals in Moscow and Saint Petersburg, the ramps themselves evolved into lavish affairs, some Ice Slides stretching several city blocks. The largest of these ramps could accommodate up to thirty sleds at a time, and torches were lit along the perimeter to allow for nighttime descents.

Despite what one might think, the Ice Slides produced remarkably few broken bones. The reputation of these rides grew so fast that they became known throughout the rest of the thrill-seeking world as Russian Mountains. There is also evidence that the Russians were the first to turn the whole shebang into a year-round affair, with wheeled carts and ice-free ramps.

The French Grooved Track

The French are given credit for the first significant constructions that featured rolling stock. In 1817,

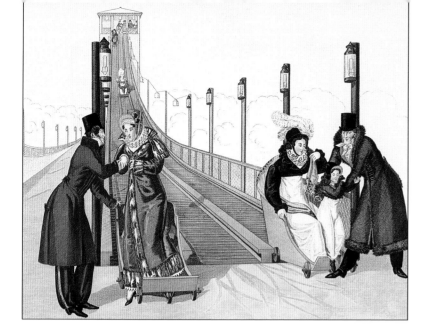

dubiously titled *Race Course* boasted cars that traveled around a circular track at the gentle speed of 10 miles per hour (16kph). This unfortunate distaste for high-velocity entertainment might have meant the end for the roller coaster's development. But thankfully, fate intervened in the form of one man by the name of La Marcus A. Thompson.

An American Revolution

Born in 1848 in Jersey, Licking County, Ohio, young La Marcus Thompson showed an early aptitude for all things mechanical. By the age of twelve, he had invented and assembled a new butter churn for his mother and an oxcart for his father. After attending Hillsdale College in Michigan and graduating in 1866, Thompson worked with several enterprises that manufactured wagons and carriages. In 1875, he developed the first seamless hosiery, which proved so popular that he and a partner founded the Eagle Knitting Company to manufacture the

Left and Below: Another landmark attraction that opened in Paris the same year as the *Promenades Aeriennes* was *Les Montagnes Russes à Belleville*, or the Russian Mountains of Belleville. This ride incorporated a significant safety innovation: vehicles that were securely locked down onto the ramp via extended wheel axles and grooved guide rails, clearly seen in these two illustrations.

two such rides were opened in Paris, *Les Montagnes Russes à Belleville* and *Promenades Aeriennes*. While these rides may not have looked much like the coasters we know and love, they introduced mechanical notions that are still with us. *Les Montagnes Russes à Belleville* utilized carts with wheel axles that extended into grooved tracks, keeping the vehicles locked safely onto the ramp. A primitive cable system to pull cars to the peak, a forerunner of the chain lift, was introduced on the *Promenades Aeriennes*. Russian Mountains of one kind or another began appearing all over Europe and for several decades proved to be as popular with Europeans as the Ice Slides were with Russians. There were even some attempts at looping rides, dubbed Centrifugal Railways, but people stayed away from these questionably trouble-free attractions.

Sadly, the waning years of the nineteenth century saw these early roller coasters fall out of fashion with the public. Some traveling carnivals featured newfangled thrills, but many permanent amusement parks were shuttered. Rides manufactured in Europe during those uninspired times were rather tepid devices, such as the *Mechanical Electric Race Course*, built in 1889 in Nice, France. The

Below: As the success of France's Russian Mountains spread, designers wasted little time before tackling looping coasters, then known as Centrifugal Railways. Apparently, though, the public had little interest in such diversions; the few Centrifugal Railways that were built didn't last long. And when, in 1865, there was one last effort made to erect a Centrifugal Railway at the Circus Napoleon, the ride's vehicle derailed on its first trial run. Thankfully, local law enforcement shut it down permanently posthaste.

new product. But it was while convalescing from nervous exhaustion in Arizona that La Marcus decided to apply his considerable ingenuity to creating amusement devices.

Thompson's thinking had no doubt been affected by the national fame and financial success of the *Mauch Chunk Switchback Railroad*. The gravity-powered *Switchback Railroad* began life in 1827 as a way to haul anthracite coal down from mines in Pennsylvania's Mt. Jefferson to the Lehigh River at Mauch Chunk. It eventually grew into an 18-mile (29km) loop of track that traveled between Mt. Jefferson and the neighboring Mt. Pisgah. This engineering breakthrough served its utilitarian function beautifully, but garnered even more attention as a tourist attraction; people traveled from around the country to ride the *Switchback Railroad* at a dollar a trip. By 1873, the *Switchback Railroad*'s cargo consisted exclusively of paying customers. The highlight of the otherwise sedate eighty-minute excursion was its final

leg, a shockingly rapid descent down the side of Mt. Jefferson.

Though inspired by this proto-coaster, Thompson's initial effort would prove to be remarkably tame compared to the *Switchback Railroad* experience. Thompson was not even the first to receive a patent for an inclined-plane railway, but he was the first to both earn a patent (number 310,966) *and* actually build a working "Roller Coasting Structure," as it was identified on patent documents.

The *La Marcus Thompson Switchback Railway* opened at New York's Coney Island on June 13, 1884, a red-letter date in coaster history. This charmingly modest ride featured two straight, parallel tracks, with raised platforms at either end. Several riders would board a car on one platform, coast down the gently sloping hills, and disembark at the other end. Attendants would push the car onto the opposite platform, and everyone would climb back on for the return trip. By today's standards, it wasn't exactly what you'd call a scream

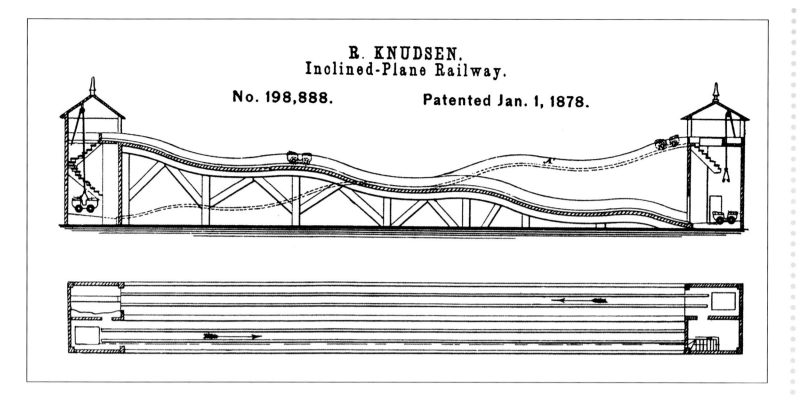

R. KNUDSEN.
Inclined-Plane Railway.

No. 198,888.   Patented Jan. 1, 1878.

Left: A person named R. Knudsen received a patent for the "Inclined-Plane Railway" in 1878, predating La Marcus Thompson's own 1885 patent for a "Roller Coasting Structure." But, for "reasons unknown," according to coaster historian Robert Cartmell, an example of Mr. Knudsen's creation was never built.

Page 18 Top: One of Coney Island's glorious amusement parks was Steeplechase, designed by George C. Tilyou, the Walt Disney of his era. Pictured in this illustration are a number of Steeplechase's attractions, including its most famous, and one of the most unusual coaster-like rides ever conceived, the *Steeplechase Ride* (upper right). Passengers would race astride wooden, twin-saddled horses, "galloping" over the oval course to the finish line. After being destroyed by one of the many fires that plagued Coney Island in the early 1900s, *Steeplechase Ride*'s eight wooden horses were replaced with four metal versions.

Page 18 Bottom: Three thrill-seekers-in-training brave the front row on an old "side-friction" coaster (so named because of the upright side rail that bracketed their cars). Lakemont Park's *Leap The Dips*, in Altoona, Pennsylvania, is one of the very few side-friction coasters still in operation today.

machine, but the *Switchback Railway* was almost unimaginably popular. Each ride cost a nickel, and Thompson was grossing $600 *a day*. Ever find yourself complaining about a long wait for the latest supercoaster? Folks stood in line for *three hours* for the privilege of a trip on this 600-foot- (183m) long, 6-mph (9.5kph) ride. Almost immediately, Thompson began fielding offers from parks around the world to purchase their own *Switchback Railways*, and competitors began to enter the fray. La Marcus' humble device was like a flame to gunpowder; the evolution of the modern roller coaster became explosively rapid.

Charles Alcoke of Hamilton, Ohio, constructed a similar ride at Coney Island, but he built his railway as a continuous circle. Philip Hinckle of San Francisco upped the ante even further by adding a hoist to his ride that pulled the cars to a more daring height, finally offering some bona fide thrills. While these efforts certainly threatened Thompson financially, they also forced him to continue refining his vision for the roller coaster. Between 1884 and 1887, he pushed the concept in many new direc-

tions and was rewarded with an additional twenty-nine patents. Thompson also began collaborating with James A. Griffiths, another designer, and John Miller, his chief engineer, on what would be his masterpiece: the *Scenic Railway*.

Thompson's revolutionary *Scenic Railways* were both state-of-the-art roller coasters and elaborate dark rides. Besides traveling over several hills, trains would journey through dazzling artificial environments: exotic Asian and Egyptian tableaus, biblical spectacles, great historical disasters, and caverns populated with devils and dragons. Dramatic lighting and mechanical effects were electronically triggered by the passing cars to the mesmerized delight of the *Railways*' passengers. These rides were the *Space Mountains* of their day, showcasing the limits of technology and creativity, and they were even more popular than his *Switchback Railways*. The first *Scenic Railway* opened in 1887 on Atlantic City's famous boardwalk and almost overnight became the world's most renowned amusement attraction. More than 2,800,000 people rode one of Thompson's *Scenic Railways* at the

Opposite: This Paradise Park is yet another of America's many "golden age" amusement parks that met its sad demise long ago.

1908 Franco-British Exposition. As a measure of this ride's impact, the U.S. Patent Office in Washington, D.C., refers to all roller coasters as "scenic railways" to this very day. With his precedent-setting achievement, Thompson wrote himself into the history books; Newton may have discovered gravity, but La Marcus Thompson harnessed it like nobody else before him. To thrill seekers everywhere, he will forever be known as the Father of Gravity.

A near-hysteria for roller coasters swept America like a brushfire, and new companies were formed to meet the demand. Griffiths left Thompson to join forces with designer George C. Crane, creating the Griffiths and Crane Scenic and Gravity Railway Company. In 1904, the Philadelphia Toboggan Company opened its doors for business. And after Thompson's retirement in 1915, John Miller continued to pioneer many safety innovations that allowed roller coasters to grow into the wild rides we cherish today.

Right: This funky steel-railed attraction, with a triangular track design, operated in Paris, France, in 1956, apparently predating what is considered the first real steel roller coaster, Disneyland's *Matterhorn Bobsleds,* which opened in 1959.

The first "golden age" of roller coasters had begun, and the Roaring Twenties were indeed roaring. The race was on to devise the most gut-wrenching roller coaster possible. Along with the highly influential Miller, designers such as Frederick Church, Frank Prior, Harry Baker, Arthur Looff, Fred Pearce, and Harry Traver created bigger and faster rides, some of which were truly horrific. Traver is notorious for designing the legendary Crystal Beach *Cyclone* (1927–1946), a ride so violent it is considered to be the most terrifying roller coaster ever built.

At the height of this golden age, as many as fifteen hundred roller coasters were rumbling across the country. It was a good time to be alive. But the roller coaster's early glory was short-lived: when the nation was swallowed up by the Great Depression, the tide turned dramatically for the country's amusement parks. Many closed for good. Those parks that remained began a decades-long slide into decrepitude. If fire didn't finally destroy a park, real-estate speculators did. One amusement resort after another fell under the cruel blow of the wrecking ball, only to see an

Left: Back in the coaster's first heyday, roller coasters were a staple of innumerable seaside amusement boardwalks, like this pier-supported racing coaster built far out over the water.

Below: California's Santa Cruz Beach Boardwalk is one of the surviving traditional coastal amusement parks and its *Giant Dipper* woodie is a twister with few equals.

apartment complex, strip mall or a shopping center rise from its ashes.

It is almost a miracle that any roller coasters have survived at all.

When it opened in 1955, Anaheim's Disneyland single-handedly resurrected and redefined the concept of an amusement park, becoming the first such place to be called a theme park. Four years later, Disneyland planted the seeds for the roller coaster's renaissance with its unveiling of the celebrated *Matterhorn Bobsleds*. Engineered by the Arrow Development Company, the *Bobsleds'* remarkable tubular steel track and polyurethane-wheeled rolling stock brought the roller coaster into the atomic age and paved the way toward the exalted steel coaster cornucopia we enjoy today. But thirteen years would pass after the *Bobsleds'* premiere before the coaster's dramatic comeback truly began.

Kings Island, now a part of the Paramount Parks group, opened in 1971 in Cincinnati, and its original owner, Taft Broadcasting, soon hired the late, great John Allen to build them a wooden roller coaster. Allen, president of the Philadelphia Toboggan Company since 1954, created *The Racer*, a gloriously white pair of sleek out-and-back coasters that still qualifies as one of the most beautiful thrill rides in the world. On April 29, 1972, *The Racer* opened to the public, and it was more than just a resounding success; it touched a nerve. Americans woke from their collective slumber and rediscovered the roller coaster. *The Racer* was fast, smooth, and, perhaps most important, telegenic, and it received the kind of press coverage that political candidates would kill for. Parks around the country began to commission their own coasters, and once again, the race to build the biggest ride took off. The success of John Allen and

Opposite: These sensuously curving rails once carried trains over a woodie at San Francisco, California's Playland Park.

Left: New Jersey's Palisades Amusement Park was home to a variety of roller coasters during its long history, beginning in 1898 and ending in 1971. Today, high-rise condominiums stand in place of the great park. What a shame.

Below: The love for high-speed hilarity translates into almost any language. Take, for example, this Taiwanese coaster, circa 1954.

his *Racer* ushered in the roller coaster's second golden age, for which we will always be in his debt.

Allen, who died on August 17, 1979, should have been able to witness the kinds of rides that followed in his wake: inverted coasters, stand-up coasters, linear induction motor coasters, and on and on and on. The roller coaster is enjoying a surge of popularity that rivals its early fame, and that popularity shows no signs of abating. Today, some several hundred coasters operate worldwide—still a far cry from their numbers so many decades ago—but each summer sees the total grow by several dozen, and we can rest assured that this second golden age is just getting started.

EVERYBODY LOVES A WOODIE—WOODEN COASTER RIDES

CHAPTER 2

The roller coaster "genus" encompasses an exotic variety of distinct species, and the simplest way to begin examining these mechanical animals is to divide them into two basic groups: steel coasters and wooden coasters (more affectionately known as woodies).

To the casual observer, these classifications would seem to indicate the materials used for their structural supports. But as the accredited coaster biologist well knows, wood and steel coasters are so designated because of their rail systems. Like the first of their breed, Disneyland's *Matterhorn Bobsleds*, steel coasters employ pipelike rails and vehicles equipped with polyurethane wheels, whereas the traditional woodie carries its metal-wheeled trains over a roadbed of laminated wood planks.

As a matter of fact, a fair number of woodies, both old and new, actually use iron girders rather than lumber to buttress their courses, like Indiana Beach's *Hoosier Hurricane*, the *Great White* on the Wild Wheels Pier in New Jersey, and the venerable *Cyclone* at New York's Coney Island. And several "steel" coasters ride atop timber support structures (but we'll get to those oddities in the next chapter).

That said, we can move on to take a closer look at what many aficionados consider the purest form of the roller coaster: the woodie.

Out-and-Back Woodies

Woodies generally come in one of two flavors: out-and-back or twister. As one might guess, out-and-back coasters do just that: they charge out, turn around, and charge back. Straightforward in design, these rides are typically a near-linear progression of summits and valleys engineered to deliver plenty of what the thrill-seeking community calls airtime, that moment when we fly over each peak and are lifted out of our seats by negative gravitational forces, or negative Gs. As far as the diehards are concerned, the higher we go and the longer we're airborne, the better.

The Racer at Paramount's Kings Island is the attraction that begat the second golden age of coasters. It's a textbook example of an out-and-back coaster (more precisely, two mirrored examples) and twice as sweet because its paired trains don't just race; one faces forward and the other backward. Ditto for *The Racer*'s siblings, *Thunder Road* at Paramount's Carowinds in North Carolina and *Rebel Yell* at Paramount's Kings Dominion in Virginia. John Allen, the designer of *The Racer*, also created the *Great American Scream Machine* for Six Flags Over Georgia and the *Screamin' Eagle* for Six

Left: U.S. coastlines were once peppered with innumerable seaside amusement boardwalks, but few have survived. Perhaps the most revered of the remaining beachfront parks is California's Santa Cruz Beach Boardwalk, home to the absolutely splendid *Giant Dipper*. Although the ride's dimensions and speed are not record-breaking, this golden age woodie, designed by Arthur Looff, has been regularly appearing on top ten lists since its debut in 1924.

Flags St. Louis, two L-shaped out-and-back coasters that are also masterworks of this genre.

Shivering Timbers

A more recent edition to the out-and-back brigade is *Shivering Timbers*, a towering, 1-mile- (1.6km) long wonder designed by Custom Coasters International (CCI). Ranked as America's third-largest woodie

when it debuted in 1998, *Shivering Timbers* earned instant, copious praise and took an unpretentious family-owned park called Michigan's Adventure from relative anonymity to national celebrity.

The coaster's lift hill tops out at 125 feet (38m) and drops down 120 feet (36.5m) at a hair over 53 degrees, good enough to send its Philadelphia Toboggan Company trains flying along at 65 miles per hour (104.5kph). The second and third hills are nearly as mouthwatering: 100 feet (30.5m) at 51.5 degrees and 95 feet (29m) at 50 degrees. Those treats are followed by a fourth, 50-foot (15m) drop and a gorgeous, swooping U-turn at the coaster's far end. The last half of the voyage is a rapid-fire series of bunny-hop hills, but there's an unexpected surprise, too: a section of "trick-track" that pays homage to an element made infamous by coaster designer Harry Traver many decades ago. Traver sometimes tortured riders by undulating the rails back and forth along an otherwise straight segment, causing the train to lurch from side to side. *Shivering Timbers*' trick-track is far less brutal than I imagine Traver's must have been, but it's a clever touch nonetheless.

Accepted roller coaster wisdom dictates the following:

if you want bushels of airtime and the wildest possible ride, head directly for the last row of the last car, no matter what type of machine—wood or steel—you're boarding. With the rest of the train acting as a kind of whip, the caboose gets snapped, crackled, and popped with maximum intensity. Certainly, *Shivering Timbers* delivers a virtuoso performance for every member of its captive audience and its back-row ride is mighty fine, but many will agree that this coaster shines most brightly when ridden in the very front row....

With the rest of the train behind us, the slow climb over the top of the lift offers a moment to savor the view—and what a view it is: two parallel rails, perfectly straight, curling over immense constructions of latticed wood. But it isn't long before the rear cars catch up with us and down we plummet. Thundering into the first valley at superhighway speed and soaring over that second 100-foot (30.5m) hill, something magical happens: angels slide their tender hands under our posteriors and carry us aloft, gentle as a feather. And there they hold us for what seems like several seconds until we are well into the next descent. Those angels hang right in there, repeating their negative-G interventions on the second hill...and the third... and the fourth. Smooth as silk and long-lasting, it's airtime heaven.

Diving into the U-turn, then flying up and to the left, we hightail it down into the home stretch, tipping this way and that over the trick-track, hurtling under support beams, rampaging over the bunny hops, and

Left: One of the most photogenic coasters is Six Flags Over Georgia's *Great American Scream Machine*, an out-and-back woodie. As seen here, a train is poised to vault over the final set of camelback hills. This particular out-and-backer is L-shaped, rather than the more traditional sort, like *Shivering Timbers*, which simply travel in a single direction to the far end of the course, turn around, and return.

Second Largest Racing Coaster in U. S. at Long Beach, California.

Giant Racer, Coney Island, N. Y.

GIANT RACER

Cleveland

floating, always floating, right out of our seats over every last hill. With momentum to spare, the train surges into a double-helix finale, careening upward, slamming hard to the left, circling around and around, and finally coming to a halt. Simply miraculous.

Twisters and Cyclones

As opposed to out-and-back coasters, twisters put more emphasis on high-speed turns, banked plunges, and whirlpooling spirals, with layered courses that worm in and out of their own structures. The blue-ribbon winners in this category are so complex that it requires several rides to fully decipher their layouts.

The world's most famous twister, and likely the world's most famous roller coaster for that matter, is undoubtedly New York's Coney Island *Cyclone*. Designed by Vernon Keenan and built by the Harry C. Baker Company in 1927 (the same year Harry Traver's fiendish Crystal Beach *Cyclone* began its brief tenure), the C.I. *Cyclone*—now a national landmark—stands proudly as the last operating coaster from Coney Island's early glory days. But don't let its advanced age fool you—this 85-foot- (26m) tall,

3,000-foot- (914m) long woodie remains one of the most gleefully ferocious coasters on the planet.

Anyone who takes a backseat trip on the *Cyclone* will have a better appreciation for the term "crash-test dummy." Before we've crested the lift hill, the front of the train is already roaring down the *Cyclone*'s delectably steep initial dive, hauling everything behind it up and over with ruthless abandon. From that point on, we rocket over an appalling tangle of track—nine drops and six curves, all told—at a top speed of about 60 miles per hour (96.5kph). Good thing the vintage trains are padded like Barcaloungers; we're pounded in every direction—up and down, left and right—for the longest ninety seconds of our lives.

It's no wonder that this sublime thug of a twister has inspired a number of respectful imitations: Six Flags AstroWorld's *Texas Cyclone*, Six Flags Over Georgia's *Georgia Cyclone*, Six Flags Magic Mountain's *Psyclone*, Six Flags Great America's *Viper*, and Six Flags New England's *Cyclone*, among others. Many contend that the *Georgia Cyclone* is as good as or better than the original, but there's no doubt that the "Brooklyn Bomber" still holds its own against twisters nearly twice its size. Long may it run.

Right: Well into the 1960s, Coney Island was still packed wall-to-wall with amusement attractions. From far left is the sky-scraping *Parachute Drop*, the *Thunderbolt* coaster, and poking in from the right, the *Tornado*. The *Parachute Drop*'s tower remains, but only as a silent reminder of Coney Island's former grandeur. The *Thunderbolt* was torn down in November of 2000 to make room for KeySpan Park, the home of minor league baseball's Brooklyn Cyclones.

Below: Beyond its amusement attractions, Coney Island also became internationally celebrated as the birthplace of Nathan's Famous, the mother of all hot dog stands.

Late-twentieth-century twisters have indeed grown tremendously in stature, like Six Flags Over Texas' *Texas Giant*, a woodie that outmeasures the *Cyclone* in every respect. Happily, the *Texas Giant*, designed by Curtis D. Summers and debuted in 1990, is one of the exceptional megatwisters that defies the maxim "less is more." A veritable behemoth at 143 feet (43.5m) in height and 4,920 feet (1,500m) in length, this coaster starts off with a bang but really fires on all cylinders for the latter half of its journey, a rip-roaring airtime extravaganza that puts the *Texas Giant* in a league all its own.

Size is rarely an issue for first-class twisters, though, and Six Flags Marine World's *Roar!* in Vallejo, California, is a case in point. Designed by Great Coasters International, Inc. (GCI), this stellar attraction is less than 100 feet (30.5m) tall, but its single-bench articulating cars—a GCI creation—dance, leap, and coil over a voluptuous maze of track that simply defies description. Once the cars climb over the lift hill, there's nary a level section of rails until they reenter the station. Twisters don't come any more twisted than this insane pleasure.

Great Coasters International, Inc. (GCI)

Led by designers Michael L. Boodley and Clair Hain Jr., this relatively new wooden roller coaster supplier burst onto the scene in 1996 with Hersheypark's *Wildcat* in Hershey, Pennsylvania. *Wildcat*'s deliciously convoluted layout crisscrosses over and under itself in a sensuous maze of curving drops and swooping turns, harking back to classic twisters built during the early decades of the twentieth century. GCI followed up that remarkable work of art with an equally delightful pair of rides dubbed *Roar!*, one for Six Flags America outside Washington, D.C., and the other for Six Flags Marine World in Vallejo, California. The slightly more aggressive *Roar!* at Marine World features GCI's retro-styled Millennium Flyer train, a gorgeous conveyance that recalls the coaster's first golden age. In 1999, this up-and-coming outfit created a fantastic pair of intertwined, dueling woodies called *Gwazi* for Busch Gardens Tampa in Florida, and for 2000, GCI returned to Hersheypark to build America's first dueling/racing woodie pair, dubbed *Lightning Racer*.

GCI started off with a bang, and their coasters are getting better and better.

GhostRider

Some woodies defy strict categorization by combining twister and out-and-back features into one complete package. *GhostRider*, Custom Coasters International's tour de force, which blazes through the skies above Knott's Berry Farm in southern California, is just such a device, with enough rump-raising hills and frantic track twists to satisfy every predilection. As an added bonus, this woodie boasts a most imaginative legend: a restless Wild West phantom is said to lurk within the park's long-abandoned Calico Mine. When we dare to take a trip in the mine's old "ore cars," the spook comes out of hiding for a high-speed haunting....

Departing the *GhostRider* "Mining Company" headquarters, we dip and rumble around a wide sweeping turn, a tasty hors d'oeuvre before the main lift hill is served. After chugging skyward alongside the loading station and through the structure of an elevated turn, we race over the top and hurtle down a 51-degree, 108-foot (33m) precipice, veering to the left beneath a tangle of wood. By the time we reach the bottom of this primary descent, we're traveling at 60 miles per hour (96.5kph), with the coaster's southern yellow pine boards tearing by all around us. Grinding along in a completely perpendicular direction, we rise up and dive back down only to soar up again to the top of the first turnaround, a swooping 180-degree course correction similar to the far turn on the awesome *Shivering Timbers*.

Plunging and scrambling toward the lift hill, our banshee-equipped mine train surges to the right and leaps up onto a flat, high-rise turn above the loading station. This funky bit of business stands in stark contrast to the first turnaround, but it serves as a brief moment to stop screaming and inhale

Page 31: *Roar!*, at Six Flags Marine World in Vallejo, California, looks as dazzling as it rides. With retro-styled, single-bench articulating cars dashing over an endless landscape of sweeping, banking drops, this *Roar!* is even more fun—but just a bit—than its near twin at Six Flags America in Largo, Maryland.

Opposite: Knott's Berry Farm's *GhostRider* really puts the wild in "Wild West." Combining the best features of both a twister and an out-and-back coaster, *GhostRider* just about does it all. And if you think the first half of the ride is a hoot, wait until the second half; it gets even *better*.

Left: *GhostRider's* ore car–themed trains growl down a camelback hill as it heads for the first turnaround, a dazzling 180-degree swoop turn.

properly. After a midpoint brake we move right on to the second half of *GhostRider's* 4,533-foot- (1,382m) long mayhem, where this multilevel woodie gets downright ornery.

The last act begins with a severe, curving power dive off the brake run, an ejector-seat shocker of a surprise. Our ore cars are once again galloping at a furious pace, and as we hurtle over the warped rails, we're whistling into the vertical supports and cross beams of the upper roadway. As we sprint through this lumber labyrinth, it seems as though we're gaining speed. Charging out to the far end of the course, we crash around to the right beneath the swoop turn. The train drops and rises, bounding over yet another airtime-producing hump, then hustles into an undulating vortex, another classic CCI coup de grace. Rampaging clockwise, the cars churn down and back up, fighting hard to break free from this circular corral. Yippee-ki-*yay*!

Sadly, it all comes to an end as we scoot out of the helix, make a 90-degree turn, and slide into the final brake run. After just a single encounter with this supernaturally endowed woodie, there is no doubt in our minds: this coaster is the ghost with the *most*.

Speed Racers

It wasn't long after the woodie's early development that coaster designers threw in another adrenaline-boosting component: the thrill of competition. Side-by-side racing coasters have been on the scene for decades and though few of the earliest are still with us, Pennsylvania's Kennywood, a living museum of scream machine history, includes its own *Racer*, a John Miller–designed magnum opus that has been enchanting thrill seekers since 1927. Along with its heritage, the ingenious *Racer* is

remarkable for another reason: its course is one continuous stretch of track. Leave from one side of the station and you'll arrive on the other. Even more delightful, the Kennywood *Racer*'s two trains run so closely together that long-limbed adults can reach across and touch the fingertips of the opposing cars' riders.

Modern wooden racers, along with those mentioned earlier, include Six Flags Magic Mountain's *Colossus* and Six Flags Great America's *American*

Opposite: Designed by International Amusement Devices, Inc. in 1978, Six Flags Magic Mountain's *Colossus* is still one of the largest racers in the world, with a maximum height of 125 feet (38m) and a top speed of 62 miles per hour (100kph).

Left: The *Racer* is just one of the many reasons Pennsylvania's Kennywood is considered among the finest traditional amusement parks in the world. In operation since 1927, this clever racing woodie is actually one long, single track, not two separate parallel tracks.

Eagle, two massive duos that are among the tallest in the world. In North America, there's the monstrous *Le Monstre* at Canada's La Ronde Amusement Park in Montreal, Quebec. South of the U.S. border, Mexico City's La Feria contains the impressive *Serpiente De Fuego*. Across the Atlantic, in England riders can go head-to-head on Blackpool Pleasure Beach's *Grand National*. And in Spain, Universal's Port Aventura includes *Stampida*, an awesome racing twister that intertwines with *Tomahawk*, a smaller out-and-backer, making for one incredible snarl of timber.

Racers by definition are either entirely parallel, like Magic Mountain's *Colossus*, or mirrored, like Kings Dominion's *Rebel Yell*. But double-tracked woodies also come in another form: dueling coasters. In 1998, Six Flags Kentucky Kingdom introduced this concept by installing the 75-foot- (23m) tall *Twisted Twins*, a pair of twisters that run over completely independent courses. "Lola" and "Stella," as the pair are lovingly referred to, don't simply race; they storm right at each other for several near-miss "collisions" during their more than 2,600-foot- (792.5m) long catfight.

Right: Lola and Stella, the two dueling darlings of Six Flags Kentucky Kingdom's *Twisted Twins* (originally called *Twisted Sisters*), run right at each other for a number of near-miss "collisions" as they twist and shout their way over two almost entirely unique courses.

Busch Gardens Tampa took the dueling coaster concept to even greater heights in 1999 by unleashing *Gwazi*, a 90-foot- (27.5m) tall GCI-designed twosome that stuffs a number of bracing flybys into its wildly contorted paths. GCI didn't stop there: one year later, the company generated the first racing *and* dueling coaster for Pennsylvania's Hersheypark—a sensuous blockbuster called *Lightning Racer*.

Hersheypark's *Lightning Racer*

Lightning Racer wasn't the first working partnership between the two entities; Hersheypark was where GCI had its coming-out party in 1996 with *Wildcat*, a transporting twister that still shows up on top-ten lists. But this new racing/dueling duet, outfitted with GCI's Millennium Flyer single-bench articulating trains, nearly puts *Wildcat* to shame....

At the far end of Hersheypark's Midway America is where we find the *Lightning Racer* and its classically inspired boarding station, which is bright white with suitably patriotic red and blue trimmings. We take the long way around to get there so that we can start at the back end and stroll along its entire length, savoring every seductive foot.

Inside the station, we're faced with a choice. To the left are the green Thunder trains, to the right the red Lightning. Makes little difference which we choose, but we do ourselves a favor and spend an extra few minutes waiting for the forward car, since this is our first ride.

As each incoming pair of trains enters the station, the winners are greeted with a hearty announcement over the loudspeakers and a flashing color-coded light. It's plenty festive and raucous enough to get those competitive juices flowing. And look at those sweet, open-front cars leading the charge.... Settling in and pulling down the lap bars, we know these snug puppies were designed by people who love what they do.

Each train drops out of the station and whistles around a turn before mounting its respective chain lift—Thunder on the inside, Lightning on the outside. Those lifts are staggered by quite a few feet, so we aren't quite "racing" yet, but we wouldn't want our attention distracted by the other cars anyway. Off to the right, we gaze down in wonder at *Lightning Racer*'s snake-pit jumble of naked yellow pine. One word: stupefying. Finally, we're at the 90-foot (27.5m) pinnacle and the race is on!

Left: This rowdy knot of lumber is just one of *Lightning Racer*'s duel zones, where the two cargo-haulers careen right at each other before meeting up again to race in parallel directions.

We plunge down a glorious fall, diving and tipping to the right. Hitting more than 50 miles per hour (80.5kph), the two trains soar all the way to ground level and motor right back up to the left, cresting another pair of staggered hills, smooth and graceful as a team of synchronized swimmers.

We race back down and each train splits off to enter the outside legs of *Lightning Racer*'s sumptuous Siphon Drops. Up and around we go, sweeping over these architecturally stunning structures, preparing to dive into the maw of a waterfall-covered tunnel. Thunder and Lightning veer toward each other, plunging closer and closer.

Hooking up at the bottom of this exquisite descent, we slam into the darkness, where a tasty little bunny hop is waiting to give our butts a solid boost. Jumping side by side over this unexpected treat, the two trains speed back into daylight and the racing starts to get hot and heavy.

Soaring through another feisty turn, we're runnin' like the wind back toward the station through what they've properly nicknamed Sideswipe Alley: up and down, left and right, careening like there's no tomorrow through the furious core of a lumber maelstrom.

Making another set of completely independent moves, both trains whip up into opposing turns alongside the lift hill for a second near-miss flyby. Around and around and then it's back down for another headlong, chaotic sprint toward the far end of the *Racer*'s course—and sprint these two most certainly do. Slashing low and mean over the ground, it feels like we haven't lost an ounce of velocity, another testament to GCI's prodigious talent.

Thunder and Lightning go at it with ever greater intensity, lashing around each other like irate anacondas. Lightning leaps over Thunder as the two trains head for the last flyby, a revolution that'll

Right: With quite a distance to go before reaching the checkered flag, *Lightning Racer*'s red Lightning train displays fluid agility as it coils through a banked turn to the left. Few coasters better characterize the expression "poetry in motion."

FINISH LINE

poise us for the dash to the finish line. Growling around these U-turns, we plow down to joust and then hasten to meet up again.

Dead ahead is the checkered flag. There's a quick dive and a rise back up to the brake run, each trainload trying to will itself to victory. It's going to be a photo finish…and the winner is—!

On *Lightning Racer*, everybody wins.

Terrain Coasters

On the largest of scales the world isn't flat, but for many of us stuck on the surface, it might as well be. So it goes for the majority of amusement parks, where the real estate is as level as the day is long. But for parks blessed with uneven topography and the imagination to take advantage of it, the doors open to the possibility of yet another type of woodie: the terrain coaster.

While terrain coasters include lift hills and sections with considerable support structures, they also adhere to the contours of rolling knolls and deep valleys to generate drama and increase the total vertical measure of their layouts. Kennywood, located on an intoxicatingly irregular site above the Monongahela River, is a terrain coaster paradise with several rides, both wood and steel, that exploit its dales and ravines to brilliant effect—and nothing exemplifies that better than Kennywood's crown jewel, the mighty *Thunderbolt*.

Starting with an old Kennywood John Miller–designed coaster called the *Pippin*, Andy Vettel threw out portions and added new track to unveil the *Thunderbolt* in 1968. It was then, is now, and likely always will be one of a kind. Among its many idiosyncrasies: the chain lift isn't encountered until well into the course, and the *Thunderbolt*'s biggest drop is its last.…

Once the boarding station's brakes are released, the *Thunderbolt* plunges forward, right down into a valley. After a turn and another ground-hugging descent, it is only then that we mount the chain lift. This 70-foot (21.5m) climb feeds us into the coaster's centerpiece, a tempestuous vortex of steep drops and tight turns that, while bruising, are mere child's play compared to what lies ahead.

Without warning, the train yanks to the left and missiles over a cliff, plummeting 80 feet (24.5m) down. We're already begging for mercy, but it's not over yet. After regaining altitude and shredding through a U-turn, we lunge into a gut-wrenching 90-foot (27.5m) dive. Seconds later, we're back in the boarding station, quivering like a bowl of Jell-O.

Left: The formidable Kennywood *Thunderbolt* rockets down a leg of the coaster's mid-course vortex, gathering steam before making two final drops into a neighboring ravine. One of the most extreme of all terrain coasters, the *Thunderbolt*'s two longest descents hit right at the very end of the ride.

Opposite: *The Legend* is based upon Washington Irving's creepy story "The Legend of Sleepy Hollow."

Custom Coasters International (CCI)

Until Custom Coasters suddenly ceased operation in 2002, this engineering company was without equal. CCI's first undertaking was the *Sky Princess*, built for the Dutch Wonderland amusement park in Lancaster, Pennsylvania, in 1992. At 53 feet (16m) tall and 1,980 feet (603.5m) long, the *Sky Princess* wasn't exactly a barn burner. But from then on, CCI became the world's pre-eminent builder of modern wooden roller coasters. The firm crafted dozens of woodies during the 1990s and a majority of them are among the finest, such as *The Raven* (Holiday World in Santa Claus, Indiana), *MegaFobia* (Oakwood park in Pembrokeshire, Wales), *Tonnerre De Zeus* (Parc Asterix in Plailly, France), *Shivering Timbers* (Michigan's Adventure in Muskegon, Michigan), *Twisted Twins* (Six Flags Kentucky Kingdom in Louisville), *Rampage* (Visionland in Bessemer, Alabama), *GhostRider* (Knott's Berry Farm in Buena Park, California), *The Villain* (Geauga Lake in Aurora, Ohio), and *The Boss* (Six Flags St. Louis), to name but a few.

Sadly, Custom Coasters president Denise Dinn decided to close up the shop that was originally started by her father, Charles Dinn—the genius behind *The Beast* and *Texas Giant*. But some of CCI's former employees have formed a new outfit called The Gravity Group and are already firing on all cylinders. And Ms. Dinn is now working with S&S Power to develop that company's own wooden coaster division.

Many will be glad to know that not all terrain coasters are equally savage. *The Raven*, a terrain snuggler at Holiday World in Santa Claus, Indiana, has a far less aggressive disposition than the *Thunderbolt* yet has managed to garner scores of "Best of Show" honors since its inaugural season in 1995; in 2000, it was selected as the world's number one wooden roller coaster by readers of *Amusement Today*, a respected industry publication. The product of a real cooperative effort between CCI and the Koch family, owners of Holiday World, this $2 million woodie amply proves that it doesn't take big budgets to create big fun....

We board *The Raven* in a distinctively foreboding Victorian mansion, appropriate for this ride's

Edgar Allan Poe–inspired theme. Once let loose, the train makes a swift U-turn, passes by the loading station, and begins to ascend the chain lift. At the pinnacle we make a hard right, and this black bird takes flight.

Plunging 86 feet (26m) into a 120-foot (36.5m) tunnel, *The Raven* beats its wings vigorously and soars onward with rowdy fervor. Smooth, quick, and nimble, this terrain coaster is all about dazzling pacing; once the action starts, it never lets up. After a speedy, banked turn over Holiday World's Lake Rudolph, our shuddering cars enter the astonishing second half of *The Raven*'s aerobatic assault with a 61-foot (18.5m) drop into the dark bowels of the park's forest. Now a full 110 feet (33.5m) below its highest peak, *The Raven* attains maximum velocity—about 50 miles per hour (80.5kph)—and goes completely haywire. Scurrying in and around the trees, the train swoops and tumbles, offering rapturous bouts of airtime.

This ride is an unqualified pleasure no matter which car you're sitting in, but if you'd like to achieve a state of higher coaster consciousness, you must try the backseat—it's incredible. At night, I've been told, *The Raven* is transformed; once you enter the woods, you're swallowed whole by pitch black darkness.

The Raven was a tough act to follow, but for the park's 2000 season, CCI and Holiday World partnered again for *The Legend*, an even taller, longer, and faster woodie that is already racking up accolades of its own; in the same *Amusement Today* poll mentioned earlier, *The Legend* was selected as the best new wooden roller coaster for that year. Not too shabby.

Bellow of *The Beast*

The mother of all terrain coasters is a ride that is as legendary as they come. On July 10, 1978, prior to its purchase by Paramount, Kings Island (located in Ohio), made an announcement that had disco-era thrill seekers dancing in the streets: construction had begun on a single-track coaster "that would break all existing records as the longest and fastest, with the two longest vertical drops."

William C. Price, then the park's general manager, stated, "Not only are the statistics of the ride awesome, but its use of the rugged natural terrain ensures that no other roller coaster tops these thrills, weaving along steep cliffs, down ravines, into four spectacular tunnels, through nine sharply banked turns, among a forest of trees, and often at treetop height."

When the coaster's proposed statistics were revealed, "awesome" was a most appropriate way to describe them. The first drop, angled at 45 degrees, would dive 135 feet (41m) right into an underground tunnel. The last major descent would stretch 141 feet (43m), sloping at 18 degrees and pouring us right into a 540-degree, banked helix. Finally, the ride would be the longest roller coaster ever conceived, covering a 35-acre (14ha) plot of land with a track length of 7,400 feet (2,255m). That's nearly a mile and a half (2.4km) long.

This yet-to-be-named monster had been designed by Charles Dinn, at that time the park's director of construction, maintenance, and engineering (and who also, by the way, once worked in a nuclear propulsion lab). He presided over an in-house team that included Jim Nickell, Al Collins, and William Reed, with outside consultation provided by renowned Philadelphia Toboggan Company designer John Allen. Dinn stated, "We studied every major coaster in the country and incorporated the best features of each one into our new ride…. This project has been a labor of love for us all and our final product will be the dream of every coaster designer."

Early in 1979, the park owners came up with a name and went so far as to poll die-hard coaster riders to see what they thought of the potential moniker. The reactions were just what they had hoped to elicit:

"Something that's out in the woods and kind of sitting there and terrifying."

"That name would really…make me want to get on it."

"It says, 'This isn't going to be…cotton candy and snow cones; this is going to be SOMETHING."

With that supportive feedback, they made it official: this record-demolishing woodie would be known as The Beast.

Left: Even from well above Paramount's Kings Island in Ohio, *The Beast* is almost entirely hidden beneath an impenetrable forest at the park's far end. All that can be seen here are the peaks of the woodie's two lift hills. The multiloop Arrow Dynamics–designed *Vortex* (in the foreground), on the other hand, is hard to miss.

Above: The lead car of *The Beast* proudly boasts a three-dimensional relief of the coaster's logo. According to the park, *The Beast* has had well over 33 million riders since its opening.

Opposite: Diving down the first plunge of *The Beast*, riders get a fleeting look at this staggering terrain coaster's world-renowned finale: a 141-foot- (43.0m) long, 18-degree slope that feeds trains into a vast, partially enclosed helix. Navigated at bone-crushing velocities, *The Beast*'s climactic spiral is, in a word, unforgettable.

It took more than three years of planning and construction to bring *The Beast* to life. Built entirely by the park's own staff, the effort consumed $3.8 million; 4,300 hours of precision study to limit design tolerances to less than one-sixteenth of an inch (1.5mm); 87,000 hours of construction work; 650,000 board feet (1,534m³) of redwood lumber; 37,500 pounds (17,025kg) of nails; 82,480 bolts; 5,180 washers; and 2,432 square yards (2,033m²) of poured concrete, enough to lay down about 3.5 miles (5.5km) of two-lane highway.

On a rainy morning in early April 1979, *The Beast*'s first 2,700-pound (1,226kg), fire-engine red car was threaded onto the rails. Under the watchful eyes of six engineers, seventeen technicians, fifty-three construction workers, four managers, and assorted guests, a train slid around the first turn, rose up the first chain lift, and dived into

destiny. On Saturday, April 14, 1979, *The Beast* was officially released. Even as the years have passed and coasters have been built taller and faster, few have matched *The Beast*'s phenomenal impact. It is epic in every sense of the word.

Lurking within a dense forest at the far end of the park's Rivertown section, *The Beast* is impossible to spot until you've just about reached the point of no return. Finding your way back is as simple as following the creature's "footprints" painted on the asphalt past Kings Island's Eiffel Tower. The queue is housed in a dilapidated, abandoned mine shack and all that is visible is the first lift hill, stretching far and away into the unknown. If you want to learn more about where *The Beast* runs riot, you've got to do it the hard way....

With lap bars secured, we chug around a wide turn and start to climb. The trip to the top is a feast for the senses: the sunbathed view of the earth dropping further and further away, the spine-tingling anticipation of waiting to curl over the pinnacle, the clankity-clank of the chain lift, the pungent fragrance of creosote.

Moments before we hit the summit, the chain lift slows. Sitting in the front row, we get to soak up the thrills to come and *The Beast*'s preposterous finale: a long, shallow descent into a massive, partially covered spiral. And what's that directly below? A perilously small hole in the ground.

We rip down the first 135-foot (41m) hill directly into that appallingly narrow subterranean tunnel. We watch as riders who'd raised their arms high tuck them right back down, fearing the loss of a digit or two as we blast into the rocky maw. As we rush to the left in the tunnel's darkness, the ear-piercing screech of metal wheels grinding against the rails is deliciously echoed and amplified by the cavern's walls. We're "only" doing about 50 miles

Right: Although not classified as a terrain coaster, the absolutely gorgeous *Giant Dipper* woodie, a classic designed by Frank Prior and Frederick Church (two kings of the coaster's first golden age), uses its oceanfront location at Belmont Park in San Diego, California to dramatic effect. This beauty stood idle for years and was nearly demolished, but ultimately saved and restored by a concerted grassroots effort.

per hour (80.5kph) at this point, with still more distance to fall.

Bolting out of the first tunnel and back into daylight, we crest a second hill, flying over the top and floating out of our cushy seats. Back down into a valley, the train bucks and quivers, only to rise again and thrash to the right onto a long, covered brake run. We glide down this slope, brakes scrubbing off a little speed, but get right back into business by twisting to the right and beginning *The Beast*'s ground-hugging middle act.

From this point on, until we hit the bottom of the next lift, our cars rumble over the surface of *The Beast*'s rugged, 35-acre (14ha) turf. There are no severe drops to speak of, but with the ever-increasing acceleration, it feels like we're unwitting passengers on a runaway freight train. Swooping up and down, twisting left and right, *The Beast* charges harder and faster, burrowing below the earth a second time, wailing through a counter-clockwise curve inside this darkened shaft.

Exiting the second tunnel, *The Beast* howls on, still accelerating and nearing the conclusion of its esteemed routine. We tremble and flop like rag dolls as *The Beast* finally hits its top speed, more than 64 miles per hour (103kph), and rockets around a bend toward lift hill number two. At this point, most other coasters would have long since run out of steam, but not this one. Stop yer grinnin' and drop yer linen, 'cause here comes the helix.

Making this second deliberate climb, we have plenty of time to eyeball the massive, 540-degree vortex at the bottom of the 141-foot- (43m) long, 18-degree ramp. Looming off the port bow, it gradually comes into view as we rise above the tree line. If we can tear our attention away from the spaghetti bowl of lumber ahead of us, this is our last chance to enjoy the woodsy scenery before the

Below: Both Paramount's Great America (Santa Clara, California) and Paramount's Kings Dominion (Doswell, Virginia) sport woodies called *Grizzly*, but PKD's model, pictured here, is a superior ride, especially at night. During this *Grizzly*'s gallop, riders speed through a tunnel with an action-packed surprise hidden inside.

Opposite: Crafted to look like the woodies of old, *California Screamin'*, the steel roller coaster at Disney's California Adventure, is anything but old-fashioned. Designed by Intamin, this state-of-the-art coaster features a linear induction motor launch and a vertical loop within its extravagantly long 6,072-foot (1850.7m) course.

train inches toward the final apex, edges over, and makes a left-hand turn. We're just seconds away from experiencing what is perhaps the world's most exhilarating coaster wrap-up.

Because the descent angle is relatively small, there's no immediate burst of speed. Instead, we start gradually, leisurely moving faster and faster—20, 30, 40 miles per hour (32, 48, 64.5kph) and building steam. Finally, we lunge beneath the upper layer of the helix. The track begins to bank and the bedlam begins.

The train quakes, certain to fly apart, as we pound into the spiral. We're traveling at about 51 miles per hour (82kph), but with the wooden beams of the helix's shed whipping by just inches from our fragile skulls, it feels like twice that speed. Around and around we go, lateral G-forces smashing us against the right side of the car. The furious turbulence is relentless.

Exploding out of the semi-circular tunnel, we hurtle toward the elevated section of this massive revolution. Only halfway through the blistering onslaught, the train jolts onto the upper level of the helix and dives back down for more. Screaming back into the shed, we regain speed and slam through the last covered portion of the spiral, *The Beast* heaving and lurching with animalistic rage.

Before the ride becomes more than any mortal can take, it's over. The train slides down

a final brake run alongside the first lift hill and comes to a stop. Ah, what a shame—but we've been fortunate enough to spend well over four minutes in the company of one of the greatest wooden roller coasters the world will ever know. Thundering through that climactic maelstrom ranks as one of life's finest pleasures, something to be shared with the people we love.

Hard as it may be to believe, *The Beast* is still the world's longest wooden roller coaster more than two decades after its introduction. In 1999, Kings Island heralded *The Beast*'s twentieth anniversary by taking note of its crowd-pleasing performance record: its three trains had racked up a combined odometer total of more than 494,362 feet (150,681m), equivalent to circling the planet twenty times. And by that year, *The Beast* was able to boast of carrying more than 31,615,839 guests on its amazing journey.

Some folks insist that nothing will never equal the raucous, barnstorming satisfaction of the traditional woodie. If you're one of them, you have no cause for concern. Thanks to the efforts of CCI, GCI, the Roller Coaster Corporation of America, CoasterWorks!, and many others, the wooden roller coaster continues to thrive in this age of predominantly metal monsters. (Very recently, Kings Island itself installed a woodie that broke several of *The Beast*'s records, but we'll get to that one in a later chapter).

There's no question, though, that the closing years of the last millennium witnessed an incredible wave of technological innovation that has been applied predominantly to steel coasters, and that wave shows no signs of cresting anytime soon. Turn the page and get ready to see how far the contemporary roller coaster has evolved beyond its humble lumber roots.

HOT WHEELS ON STEEL COASTERS

CHAPTER 3

If we were to draw a family tree for the steel roller coaster, we'd begin with a single trunk called Disneyland's *Matterhorn Bobsleds*, circa 1959. But from that trunk, we'd need to begin drawing branches. And then more. And then more still, because today the steel coaster comes in a mind-blowing profusion of styles. Just like woodies, steel coasters can be identified as twisters, out-and-backers, racers, dueling coasters, and terrain coasters—but that's just the beginning. To further complicate things, the steel genus also encompasses mine trains, stand-up coasters, suspended swinging coasters, inverted coasters, floorless coasters, launched coasters, shuttle coasters, flying coasters, and more. To the uninitiated, it's a tad bewildering.

A Gold Mine

Let's jump back to the 1960s, not long after the *Matterhorn Bobsleds*' pioneering premiere. Arrow Development (now Arrow Dynamics, Inc.), as you'll recall, helped develop the *Matterhorn Bobsleds* and, having mastered the art of bending tubular steel rails, went on to create the mine train, a mild steel-railed coaster attraction that quickly became a staple at new theme parks opening around the United States. The first, *Runaway Mine Train*, was introduced at Six Flags Over Texas in 1966, and it's still one of the best running. This spunky, 2,400-foot- (731.5m) long coaster is no rocket sled, but with its three lift hills and a tunnel that burrows under a small lake, it's good fun from start to finish. Six Flags Magic Mountain's *Gold Rusher* is another choice example of the unadorned mine train.

In recent years, parks have breathed new life into the mine train formula by adding extensive themes and animated effects. Six Flags Fiesta Texas' *Roadrunner Express* takes riders on a hazard-packed journey past several attempts by Wile E. Coyote to catch his nemesis, the Roadrunner. Paramount's Kings Island created the *Adventure Express*, a 3,000-foot- (914m) long trip through streams, into volcanic tunnels, over crumbling bridges, and down a deserted mine shaft filled with creepy, crawly critters.

Although just about all mine trains are classified as "family rides," a few of these coasters were engineered as full-fledged scream machines. Missouri's Silver Dollar City has its *ThuNderaTion*, a coaster with an 81-foot (24.5m) lift hill and curves that bank up to 60 degrees. Valleyfair! in Minnesota goes *ThuNderaTion* one (or two) better with *Excalibur*, a miner that stands 100 feet (30.5m) tall and gets its trains moving at speeds as

Left: With firm grips on their harnesses, the standing passengers aboard Six Flags Magic Mountain's *Riddler's Revenge* navigate one of this massive coaster's six loop-de-looping wig-flippers.

Right: From a distance it may look like a woodie (those are indeed lumber supports), but Cedar Point's *Gemini*, a racing mega-mine-train coaster, is by definition a steel coaster, with tubular steel rails and polyurethane-wheeled vehicles.

Page 54: A yellow-and-red train of Busch Gardens Williamsburg's *Loch Ness Monster* soars through the first of its two signature intertwined inversions. "Nessie," as she's affectionately known by her many fans, is one of the most visually stunning coasters ever built.

high as 55 miles per hour (88.5kph) after making a 60-degree, 105-foot (32m) dive.

Finally, there is Cedar Point's *Gemini*, a twin-tracked mine train on steroids that was the world's tallest coaster when in opened in 1978. Riding on a mountainous wood support structure, this 3,935-foot- (1,200m) long racer starts from a height of 125 feet (38m) and makes a 55-degree drop to hustle its trains along at 60 miles per hour (96.5kph). *Gemini* also happens to be one of those rare steel coasters with lumber supports.

Loops and Curls

Arrow's most significant contribution to all that followed was Knott's Berry Farm's *Corkscrew*. Unveiled in 1975, it was the first modern roller coaster to turn riders completely upside down. The specifications for this simple coaster now seem hopelessly quaint: track length, 1,250 feet (381m); lift height, 70 feet (21.5m); ride time, seventy seconds. The *Corkscrew*'s layout fits on a plot of land only 150 by 300 feet (46 by 91.5m), but the effect this attraction had on the amusement industry is still felt today. Those dual 5-inch- (13cm) diameter pipe rails, curling through two consecutive barrel rolls, laid a path to a glorious future filled with zero-G rolls, sidewinders, cobra rolls, heartline spins, and much, much more. (The original *Corkscrew* lives on at Silverwood Theme Park in Athol, Idaho.)

In 1976, one year after the *Corkscrew* flipped its way into the history books, Magic Mountain retaliated with the *Great American Revolution*, a looping steel coaster crafted by the preeminent roller coaster designer Anton Schwarzkopf and manufactured by Intamin, AG of Switzerland. Far larger and more elaborate than the *Corkscrew*, the

Revolution somersaulted through one completely vertical loop, a jaw-dropping element that made the coaster an unbilled star of the 1977 Universal Studios SenSurround thriller, *Rollercoaster*.

Then all hell broke loose.

Major steel coasters continued to get taller, faster, longer, and loopier as amusement parks clamored for one record-breaking attraction after another. In 1978, Arrow took a great leap forward and produced one of the most beautiful roller coasters ever created: Busch Gardens Williamsburg's 114-foot- (35m) tall, 60-mph (96.5kph) *Loch Ness Monster*. This flamboyant, yellow-tracked machine careens through the park's dense green forest, over the reflective surface of the "Rhine River," and into "Nessie's" signature interlocked loops with a kinetic elegance that still takes my breath away.

That same year, Schwarzkopf and Intamin countered with Six Flags Over Texas' *Shock Wave*, a 116-foot- (35m) tall coaster with two consecutive vertical loops, and Six Flags Over Georgia's *Mind Bender*, a ride that was billed as America's first "triple-looping" coaster (truth be told, though, one of those "loops" is really just a circular, highly banked drop—the train never properly inverts).

In 1980, Arrow followed up the *Loch Ness Monster* with Worlds of Fun's *Orient Express* and upstaged Nessie by incorporating interlocking loops and a new Arrow-engineered element dubbed the Boomerang Curve, a steel knot that turns trains upside down twice before sending them back in the direction from which they came.

The frenzy has continued unabated since, with new players muscling into the game who have more tricks up their sleeves. Today's loopiest coasters—Universal's Port Aventura's *Dragon Kahn* in Spain and Terra Encantada's *Monte Makaya* in Brazil—flip us head over heels a brain-scrambling eight times.

By the early 1980s, the novelty of watching the world turn upside down while sitting in a conventional vehicle wasn't thrilling enough, and steel coaster engineers began devising new modes of transportation to keep our amygdala's flexed.

On Your Feet

Enter the stand-up roller coaster. Togo of Japan first brought the concept of a stand-up coaster to America in 1984, at Kings Island in Cincinnati. *King Cobra* featured a single vertical loop, which was 66 feet (20m) high, with a top speed of 50 miles per hour (80.5kph). A tad peculiar, but *King Cobra* was also a brave step in a new direction. With little delay, Togo was enlisted to build nearly identical stand-up coasters for two of Kings Island's sibling parks: *SkyRider* for Canada's Wonderland in 1985 and *Shockwave* for Kings Dominion in 1986. The Swiss firm Bolliger & Mabillard, Inc., got into the act in 1990 with *Iron Wolf*, built for Six Flags Great America.

A year after the *Iron Wolf* first bayed at the moon, B&M built *Vortex*, its second stand-up railrider, for Paramount's Great America in Santa Clara, California. In 1992, the company delivered its third such device, also christened *Vortex*, to Paramount's Carowinds. With those three models under its belt, B&M spent the next few years astonishing us with new innovations, but in 1996, the firm got back into the stand-up business in a major way.

When it opened that year at Cedar Point, B&M's $12 million *Mantis* simply blew away every other stand-up coaster in existence. Humbled by its four inversions and fierce positive G-forces, some folks thought that *Mantis* was about as intense as a stand-up coaster could get. They were wrong. In 1997, B&M spawned *Chang* for Six Flags Kentucky

Kingdom, which shattered several records. Not only was *Chang* longer, taller, and loopier than *Mantis*, with five inversions, its first vertical loop, standing 119 feet (36.3m) high, was the largest head-over-heels element featured on any type of coaster. Soon, however, even *Chang* would be overshadowed in stature.

Above: Cedar Point's *Mantis*, once the world's largest stand-up coaster, pummels riders with a 119-foot- (36.3m) tall vertical loop (pictured), followed by a dive loop, an inclined loop, and a corkscrewing twist.

Below: The last of Bolliger & Mabillard's mega-stand-up coasters is *Riddler's Revenge*, the longest, tallest, fastest, and most inversion-packed stand-up coaster on the globe. Throughout the 1990s, stand-up coaster records were being broken on an almost yearly basis, but since the *Revenge*'s debut, only one new B&M stand-up has been erected: Six Flags Over Georgia's *Georgia Scorcher*, with three inversions.

Riddler's Revenge

On April 4, 1998, Six Flags Magic Mountain's magnificent *Riddler's Revenge* went into operation, besting *Chang* in every respect. As you'll recall from the *Batman Forever* film, Edward Nygma, a sad-sack inventor toiling away at Wayne Industries, became quite unhinged when his proposals for a new kind of television were soundly rejected. Choosing to pursue a life dedicated to evil, he transformed himself into the Riddler and went on to terrorize Gotham City. Of course, Batman intervened and poor Eddie's nefarious schemes were ultimately thwarted—the final reel saw him locked away at Arkham Asylum. End of story...or so we thought.

Doing time at Arkham, Mr. Nygma had little to distract him from plotting his final revenge. Now that he's back on the loose, our fortunes have taken a delightful turn for the worse. A winged cone over the entrance to his new lab looks innocent enough, but it's actually another of his consciousness-scrambling NygmaTech gadgets, a tool to subdue and lure us in....

Left: Blasting up the introductory leg of a towering dive loop, *Riddler's Revenge* (next to the park's *Freefall* attraction), soars into the firmament. And that's just the first of two such twisting, high-flying inversions riders attack during this stand-up coaster's electrifying expedition.

Standing in the queue, intertwined with the back half of the *Revenge*'s course, we are right in the thick of things, with trains sometimes roaring directly overhead. And I do mean *roar*: at one point, beneath a barrel roll inversion, the sonic blast is enough to make us wince and reconsider which line we're in. Before entering the station, we can turn to the right and check out both the 156-foot (47.5m) lift hill and the jaw-dropping 124-foot- (38m) tall vertical loop, two highlights that are just a hair bigger than those found on Six Flags Kentucky Kingdom's *Chang*...and all that sky-piercing green steel is mesmerizing.

Climbing into B&M's height-adjustable stand-up harnesses is a simple process: we shimmy onto the "seat" and bring the shoulder restraints across our chests; with our feet flat on the floor, we push up with our knees until we're completely erect. The ride attendants lock the harness into position and we're ready to roll.

We begin the ascent by climbing up and threading through not one but two of the *Revenge*'s inversions. The first shadow is cast by a dive loop, the second by that massive vertical sucker. If several trains are in operation and the gods are smiling, we may get a special treat: a train that soars

Opposite: One of Bolliger &
Mabillard's first stand-up coasters,
opened in 1992, was *Vortex* at
Paramount's Carowinds. With a maximum height of 90 feet (27.4m) and a
track length of 2,040 feet (621.8m),
this 50 mile-per-hour (80.5kph) ride
tosses riders through two inversions, a
vertical loop, and the "oblique loop"
pictured here.

through the dive loop just as we pass underneath.
Once we're past the vertical loop, the rest of the
Revenge is behind us—but not for long. At the sum-
mit, the lead car tips forward, and *Riddler's
Revenge* goes critical.

Swooping to the left and falling hard, our train
races down 146 feet (44.5m) like there's no
tomorrow. We become a chorus of the damned,
thirty-two voices screaming in unison, drowned out
only by the thundering growl of a multiton vehicle
hitting 65 hell-bent miles per hour (104.5kph).

That 124-foot (38m) loop pulls us away from
the planet's surface and the world disappears in a
swirling blur. Our yelping turns from screams of terror into ecstatic release—there is nothing but the
sensation of taking flight, of breaking gravity's
shackles and soaring free. It's a transcendent
moment, one that makes us the thrill-craving
lunatics we most certainly are. Back down we
plunge, charging right into the next element, the
first dive loop. Hurtling past the base of the park's
Freefall vertical-drop ride, the train goes skyward
and inverts, twisting to the left. This second whoop-
de-do may be a tad shorter than the vertical loop,
but it's just as exhilarating.

At this point, if we've succumbed to the experience, our superegos have surrendered to our ids,
and all we want is more. And it's more we're gonna
get: plummeting out of that maneuver, the train
surges back toward the lift hill and into another dive
loop, this one hauling us up and over the chain lift.
Shrieking back toward the opposite end of the
course, the train careers into the inclined loop, and
we're head over heels for the fourth time in a row.
It's a nonstop G-force party and everyone's invited!

The wicked loop flurry is momentarily interrupt-
ed as our coach jumps a small hill and swings
around for a midcourse brake run. Sure, we can

hear a dreaded little hiss as those mechanical nas-
ties try to slow us down, but the marauding train
crashes through with defiant anger.

Standing in the last row is especially satisfying;
there's a small drop right off the run, and as the
train regains cruise velocity, it yanks us away from
this one flat section of track good and hard. That
brutal little jolt is enough to make the brake run
worthwhile. Those few seconds of uprightitude are
over—we pour directly into a bodacious barrel roll,
performing this grand maneuver as the train makes
a beeline toward the *Freefall*. Heading down into a
steeply banked curve, we fly to the left and leap over
the *Freefall*'s horizontal "run-off" track. Leaning to the
right, the track whips us through a 250-foot (76m)
spiral, turning us around for the home stretch.

We don't deserve it, but we get one last indul-
gence: a second barrel roll that tosses us like
human salad over the waiting throngs. There's a
quick turn to the right, and this sublime *Revenge*
comes to an end.

Since the *Riddler's Revenge* began its rampage,
Bolliger & Mabillard has crafted yet another stand-
up coaster, this one called the *Georgia Scorcher*.
Opened in 1999 at Six Flags Over Georgia, the
Scorcher challenges us to put our "Feet to the Fire"
as we travel at 54 miles per hour (87kph) over its
107-foot- (32.5m) tall, 3,000-foot- (914m) long,
three-inversion course. Though it doesn't come
close to matching the *Revenge*'s overwhelming pro-
portions, the purple and golden *Scorcher* is justly
earning kudos as a fine addition to B&M's portfolio.

Intamin has also dabbled a bit in the stand-up
kitchen, manufacturing coasters like the *7-Up
Shockwave* for Drayton Manor in Staffordshire,
England, and *Batman—The Escape* at Six Flags
AstroWorld in Texas. But the stand-up coaster may
have reached its zenith with the *Riddler's Revenge*.

Suspended Coasters

Standing above the rails makes for a mildly engaging alternative to the customary steel coaster experience. Hanging below them, on the other hand, is a different story altogether. The idea of suspending a coaster vehicle from overhead tracks is far older than one might guess; coaster historian Robert Cartmell has shed light on a patent dated October 26, 1897, by one G.W. Downey, for a suspended "pleasure railway" and notes that a suspended contraption called *Bisby's Spiral Airship* operated at The Pike in Long Beach, California, in the early decades of the twentieth century.

The first modern attempt to create a suspended steel coaster took place in 1981 at Kings Island. *The Bat*, created by Arrow, was equipped with a train of vehicles that were able to swing left and right as they soared through turns and helices. With a price tag of $3.8 million, *The Bat* was a rather dramatic piece of work; gliding over 2.9 acres (1.2ha), *The Bat*'s 2,456-foot (748.5m) course included two 100-foot (30.5m) lift hills, fifteen curves, and four spirals. Folks couldn't wait to give this new machine a whirl.

Unfortunately, most of them never got that chance. *The Bat* was plagued with technical problems (relating to what has been called an underengineered train) that kept it out of commission more often than not. Eventually, Arrow decided to go back to the drawing board, and *The Bat* was quietly dismantled.

Luckily, the suspended coaster did not die. Further engineering developments resulted in an improved version, and since 1984, when the extremely popular *Big Bad Wolf* opened at Busch Gardens Williamsburg, Arrow has installed its suspended coasters literally around the world. Canada's Wonderland is home to the *Vortex*; Japan

Right: Six Flags Magic Mountain's *Ninja* is California's only suspended swinging-train coaster. Unfortunately, only a relative handful of these types of coasters exist throughout the world. They were superseded in popularity by the fixed-train inverted coaster, a ride whose vehicles can safely travel through inversions.

has the 61-mph (98kph) *Hayabusa* at Toyko Summerland; the very *Bat*-like *Vampire* once swooped through Chessington World of Adventures in southern England; and Everland Park in Korea is where you can find the *Eagle's Fortress*.

In the United States, there is a nice selection to choose from, including Cedar Point's *Iron Dragon*, Six Flags Magic Mountain's *Ninja*, and the aforementioned *Big Bad Wolf*. The suspended coaster even made its triumphant return to Kings Island in 1993 as *Top Gun*.

At one time, Arrow hoped to include inversions in its suspended coaster designs, but the ride vehicle's free-swinging capability presented a sticky problem: if a train wasn't traveling fast enough to provide momentum to whip the cars up and over the inverted track, the cars would fall to the side, with imaginably disastrous results. Without some kind of complicated mechanical pushing apparatus as a fail-safe device, inversions were out of the question. To this day, no ride manufacturer has been able to resolve this issue, and all suspended swinging coasters remain loop-free.

Inverted Coasters

In 1992, Bolliger & Mabillard introduced its own take on the rails-above recipe with a nonswinging vehicle that was capable of executing every imaginable upside-down element and allowed riders' legs to dangle freely below the train, ski-lift style. When the first of B&M's inverted coasters opened as *Batman—The Ride* at Six Flags Great America, the planet went gaga.

During its 2,700-foot- (823m) long flight, *Batman—The Ride* includes two vertical loops, two corkscrews, and a heartline spin that thrashes the train around a 360-degree roll for several seconds of weightlessness. It was a staggering achievement and since its premiere, five more *Batman—The Ride*s, of almost identical design, have been installed at Six Flags parks around the United States (Great Adventure, Magic Mountain, St. Louis, Over Texas, and Over Georgia).

But B&M was also called upon to design custom inverted coasters, and they quickly outgrew the 100-foot- (30.5m) tall *Batman*. Cedar Point's *Raptor* broke inverted records in 1994 with a

Arrow Dynamics, Inc.

Founded in 1946 by Ed Morgan and Karl Bacon, the Arrow Development Company (forerunner of today's Arrow Dynamics) was initially just a small machine shop in Mountain View, California. The company's plans did not include a mandate to help revolutionize the amusement industry, but that's exactly what Arrow eventually did.

Early on, Arrow purchased a small "kiddieland" park as a financial investment and began to repair and refurbish the existing equipment. It wasn't long before the company began designing new rides for the little amusement center, and people began to take notice. In 1947, when the city of San Jose wanted to add a carousel to their new municipal Central Park, they turned to Arrow to create the attraction. The $3,500 San Jose Merry-Go-Round turned out to be a defining achievement.

Meanwhile a man by the name of Walter Elias Disney was formulating plans for a new kind of park, and he needed a company to help him produce the unique rides and attractions that would populate Disneyland. He saw Arrow's San Jose carousel and was so impressed by its design and craftsmanship that he called upon Arrow to build not just a merry-go-round, but a wide variety of the rides that would make Disneyland a truly groundbreaking theme park: *Snow White's Adventures*, *Peter Pan's Flight*, *Dumbo*, *The Mad Hatter's Tea Party*, and the *Casey Jr. Circus Train*. In the years to follow, Arrow would create the ride transportation systems for the *Pirates of the Caribbean*, *It's a Small World*, and the *Haunted Mansion*, among others. And in 1959, four years after the park opened, Arrow crafted the tubular steel trackwork for Disneyland's seminal *Matterhorn Bobsleds*. That innovation ignited the development of a whole new coaster species, and in 1975, Arrow reintroduced the world to the looping roller coaster, Knott's Berry Farm's double-helixed *Corkscrew*.

In the decades beyond, Arrow Dynamics has created hundreds of rides and attractions for theme parks around the world. Their flume rides, mine trains, and looping coasters are among the most successful rides ever produced, and it was Arrow that engineered the awesome *Magnum XL-200* for Cedar Point. That coaster, with its 205-foot (62.5m) lift hill, became the first of what are now known as hypercoasters.

Unfortunately, later years for Arrow were difficult. After opening its first and only "4th Dimension" coaster in 2001—*X* at Six Flags Magic Mountain in California— Arrow was acquired by S&S Power, where its legacy will live on.

Left: Riders go loop-de-looping while sampling the Arrow Dynamics–designed *Tennessee Tornado* at Dollywood theme park in Pigeon Forge, Tennessee. Opened in 1999, this custom looper climbs up the side of a mountain to fall 128 feet (39.0m) and reach a top speed of 63 miles per hour (101.4kph). And its three inversions include a 110-foot- (33.5m) tall loop.

137-foot (42m) lift hill and a top speed of 57 miles per hour (92kph). Then Busch Gardens Tampa hired B&M to create *Montu*, a 60-mph (96.5kph), Egyptian-themed beast that rises to 150 feet (46m). And in 1997, Busch Gardens Williamsburg stole the crown with what was then, and is at this writing, the world's tallest inverted coaster, the bone-chilling *Alpengeist*.

Alpengeist

Alpengeist adds roughly 45 feet (13.5m) to *Montu*'s 150-foot (46m) lift hill, maxing out at 195 feet (59.5m), and once you're pulled to that dizzying peak, a 170-foot (52m) drop sends you blasting along at the "kiss your loose articles goodbye" speed of 67 miles per hour (108kph). Among the

many perverse pleasures that follow, you'll find inverted nirvana at the top of a 106-foot- (32.5m) tall vertical loop....

From far outside the park, we can see the gargantuan lift hill towering above the treetops—it's a sight that brings tears of joy (or dismay) to our eyes. Once inside the gates, we set a course for the park's Rhinefeld Hamlet and follow the jaunty accordion music. There we find the base lodge for an Alpine ski resort. We take a good look around so as not to miss out on the many amusing touches: trail maps, a ski-rental shack, slope-condition announcements, and instructor message boards. See, the story goes like this: we're out for a day of double-black-diamond skiing, and we hop on the chairlift to the summit. But the mountain is also home to a nasty snow beast, and it doesn't take kindly to strangers.

The careful attention to detail continues inside the loading station; the gorgeous train is fitted with stowed skis in the back of each car. And the seats are cozy enough to sleep in, another Bolliger & Mabillard hallmark.

The harness goes down; the belts are buckled; the floor drops away. Straight out of the station, the chain lift begins to carry us up and over the landscape toward the park's Rhine River. Nothing beats the sensation of gazing down past your knocking knees at the ground so far below...but you'll only have a fleeting moment to enjoy it. The train makes a hard right turn and enters an exquisitely banked plunge. One hundred and seventy vertical feet (52m) later, our demonically possessed conveyance is traveling at 67 miles per hour (108kph).

All that momentum carries us directly into a mammoth Immelman inversion, named for a German stunt pilot's signature maneuver. We narrowly avoid stubbing our toes on a little ski shack as we soar again toward the heavens, and with the soles of our feet getting a little sun, the train twists to the left and dives down into another little wooden hut at the base of that 106-foot (32.5m) loop. Up and over, and it's on to the cobra roll, a pretzel twist of steel that whips us upside down twice over the Rhine River and points us toward the opposite end of the course. We savor the forces pressing us down into our seats—3.7 Gs at 58 miles per hour (93kph).

The cars race up into a high-speed curve to the left and the ride's midpoint. It's a brake run, but there's only a mild hint of a pause. The action picks right up again with a steep dive into another narrow shack. Passing underneath a footbridge, the

train rips into a frantic zero-G roll for some delectable weightlessness, soaring over the *Le Scoot* flume ride spillway.

We resist the urge to pull up our legs to our chest as the cars plow down into a snowy little crevice. The course veers to the left and the train spins up and through a menacing corkscrew element, *Alpengeist*'s final inversion. But there's one last positive-G slam: the cars swing onto their sides and navigate a high-speed, 360-degree spiral before pulling back into the station.

Below: Bolliger & Mabillard reached a new inverted coaster pinnacle with Busch Gardens Williamsburg's *Alpengeist* in 1997. This 195-foot- (59.4m) tall monster, still the tallest inverted coaster in the world, begins its ferocious attack with a spiraling 170-foot (51.8m) plunge.

Not nearly as large as *Alpengeist* but almost as spectacular are Islands of Adventure's *Dueling Dragons* in Orlando, Florida. An intertwined pair of B&M-designed inverted coasters, the *Dragons* (blue Ice and red Fire) share a common lift hill but then break away to whistle through unique flight paths. And duel they do, with several hair-raising close calls.

B&M's inverted coasters have proven to be smash hits on the international stage as well. Several can be found in Japan, including the *Raptor*-like *Orochi* at Osaka's Expoland and *Gambit*, another *Batman*-esque model at Family Land in Gotemba. Italy's Mirabilandia park in Ravenna recently pulled the wraps off *Katun*, a 164-foot- (50m) tall, 3,930-foot- (1,198m) long, six-inversion adaptation. And behind the gates at England's Alton Towers, you'll encounter *Nemesis*, one of the most lavishly—and ghoulishly—themed roller coasters in

existence. Looking every inch the extraterrestrial star of a sci-fi monster movie, *Nemesis* races at up to 50 miles per hour (80.5kph) through a fantastically disorienting course dug deep into the ground.

Vekoma Rides Manufacturing is another design firm that's been helping to sate a ravenous global appetite for inverted coasters. The company's suspended looping coaster, or SLC, as it's known among the cognoscenti, is a stock design featuring two abreast trains, a 102-foot (31m) lift hill, and a madly coiled 2,172 feet (662m) of track with five head-over-heels elements. The first of these compact machines was introduced in 1994 as *El Condor* at Wabili Flevo park in the Netherlands, and in the years since, SLCs have sprouted near and far. At several Six Flags parks, they're known as either *Serial Thriller* or *Mind Eraser*. One of the more notable Vekoma SLC's is *The Great Nor'Easter* at Morey's Pier, in New Jersey, a coaster that seems to travel within millimeters of some of the pier's neighboring attractions.

Floorless Coasters

Bolliger & Mabillard's inverted coasters alone would have been enough to ensure thrill-ride immortality, but this company isn't one to rest on its laurels. B&M's frenetic research and development continued through the 1990s, and by the closing years of the last millennium, the firm had introduced yet another steel coaster variant, the floorless coaster. Essentially, B&M took a calf-dangling inverted coaster train and reworked it to roll on top of—rather than hang beneath—a pair of tubular rails. Thus the vehicle, often referred to as a flying chair, is about as stripped-down as a coaster cargo-hauler can get—nothing but a seat and shoulder harness— making for one of the most gripping front-row excursions you'll ever experience. Imagine, if you will, that riding in a standard coaster car is like racing through the Alps in the driver's seat of a redlining Ferrari. Quite a rush, but you're sheltered by the doors, dashboard, and windshield. Now imagine that instead of sitting behind the wheel, you're perched on the car's front bumper.

Medusa

New Jersey's Six Flags Great Adventure had the privilege of introducing this new steel mutant in 1999 as part of a $42 million expansion package, a huge investment that paid for twenty-five new rides, including two pint-size coasters for the younger set. But the single most expensive item was B&M's floorless *Medusa*: 146 feet (44.5m) tall and 3,985 feet (1,214m) long, with seven inversions and a maximum velocity of 61 miles per hour (98kph). Themed as the snake-headed she-demon from Greek mythology, this novel Bolliger & Mabillard coaster has jaws dropping in awe....

It's not until we enter the station and are waiting to load that we get to see just how unique a floorless coaster really is. An arriving train pulls to a stop and retracting metal panels rise from beneath either side of the platform. Once the cars are emptied, we hop on board, pull down the harnesses, and buckle them in place. When it's all clear, those panels drop and fold away in two smooth motions. As dispatch procedures go, *Medusa*'s is definitely among the swiftest and the niftiest.

Just before the train gets moving, a pair of metal gates hanging over the tracks swing open. We glide forward and make a left-hand turn onto the lift hill. Right now, the lack of any protective shell around our lower extremities doesn't seem like much—but it will very soon.

On this early spring morning, we're headed right into the burning sun and attaining the peak, 146 feet (44.5m) up; we're looking down at the green acres of Great Adventure's neighboring wildlife drive-through park—lions and tigers and bears, oh my! The view is fleeting, but it's a beauty.

Our attention is soon wrenched away from those earthbound critters. We plummet down *Medusa*'s first fall, with the track's metal cross-sections whipping by just inches beneath the soles

Above: The world's first Bolliger & Mabillard–designed floorless coaster, Six Flags Great Adventure's *Medusa*, beckons potential riders with a towering cobra roll, just two of this incredible machine's seven inversions.

of our shoes like they wanted to chew us up and spit us out. Logic should tell us that no one would ever design a coaster capable of ripping off a limb, but right now our brains' logic circuits are totally fried. Traveling at more than 60 miles per hour (96.5kph), we're as close to any coaster rails as we'll *ever* want to get.

We slam into the base of a vertical loop and the rails bend up to grab at our Keds. With the weight of the train pulling us back and slowing us down, there's some wicked hang time past the apex of the inversion, but the pace slackens for only a moment.

Right out of that element, we soar into a 96-foot- (29m) tall dive loop. Up, up, up and bending to the right, we invert and nose-dive, nearly going sub-terranean before we surge into what is *Medusa*'s singular moment—an awesome zero-G roll or heart-line camelback, where the rails hastily twirl us upside-down at the pinnacle of a lofty hill. On any B&M looping coaster, this particular maneuver is perhaps the sweetest single treat they've bestowed upon us.

Next up is a 78-foot- (24m) tall cobra roll, never more appropriately named than it is here. We drop out of the zero-G roll and then rise into one inversion, pull out, curl to the right, get twisted upside down again, and plunge. Only the most trusting will maintain any sort of normal sitting posture with their calves so close to high-speed amputation.

A midpoint brake run allows us to make sure our toes haven't been ground into hamburger—yep, they're still there. But for a beast long given up for dead, *Medusa*'s in fine form, and she isn't through slapping us around yet.

We race off the platform and scream through a nearly 90-degree-banked spiral toward a pair of interlocked corkscrews. But we don't take them one right after another. After whipping through the

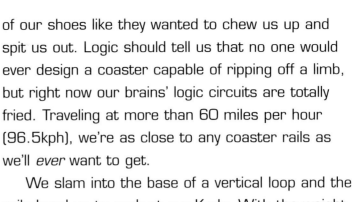

Left: Six Flags Great Adventure's *Medusa*, tosses passengers through the first leg of its cobra-roll element, having already subjected them to a vertical loop, a dive loop, and a zero-G roll or "heartline camelback."

Right: Just one year after the 1999 debut of Six Flags Great Adventure's *Medusa*, Six Flags Marine World (Vallejo, California) opened its own floorless *Medusa*. This West Coast version, while similar in many ways to its namesake, features a completely original, entirely new double-inversion element called the "Sea Serpent."

first, the train navigates a 180-degree turn and then plows through the second.

Finally, she heads for home. Back in the station with the platform magically reappearing, we can stagger free, glad to be fully intact with all limbs and digits accounted for.

The year 2000 was a very good one for floorless fans. Six Flags Marine World got its own *Medusa*, similar to its East Coast counterpart but a bit taller (150 feet [46m]) and faster (65 mph [104.5kph]) with a one-of-a-kind "Sea Serpent" double-inversion element. Down in Florida, SeaWorld Orlando unleashed *Kraken*, a 149-foot- (45.5m) tall, 4,177-foot- (1,273m) long named for the sea beast once held captive by the god Poseidon. San Antonio's Six Flags Fiesta Texas shelled out $20 million for its *Superman Krypton Coaster*, a 168-foot- (51m) tall,

70-mph (112.5kph) whopper. Last but not least, Six Flags Ohio (now Worlds of Adventure) grabbed the record for longest floorless coaster with *Batman Knight Flight*, a five-inversion model that stretches a full 4,210 feet (1,283m). And we can bet our bottom dollars that even larger floorless coasters are in the works.

Linear Induction Motor Roller Coasters

For nearly its entire history, the roller coaster has relied upon one thing for its motive force: the immutable power of gravity. After a gear-driven chain pulls the train up and over an initial hill, typically the loftiest of most courses, Newton's most famous law takes care of the rest. Even those folks

Right: These blueprint drawings amply illustrate the jaw-dropping complexity of Premier Rides' continuous-circuit LIM coasters, like *Flight of Fear* (Ohio's Paramount Kings Island and Virginia's Paramount Kings Dominion), *Poltergeist* (Six Flags Fiesta Texas), *The Joker's Jinx* (Maryland's Six Flags America) and *Mad Cobra* (Japan's Suzuka Circuitland).

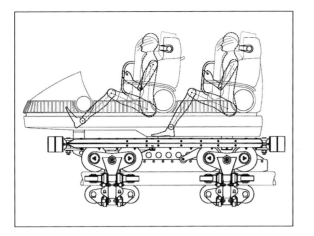

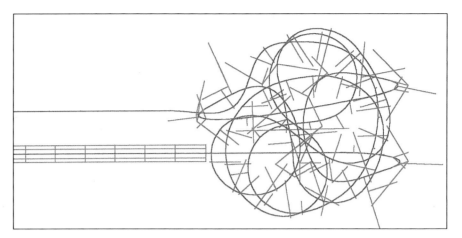

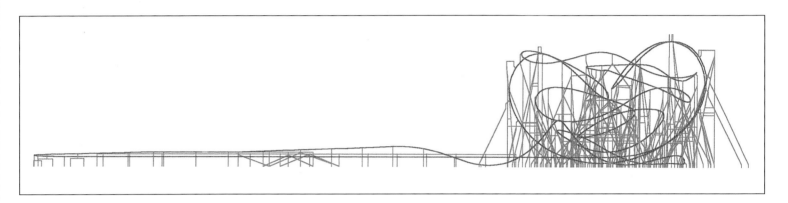

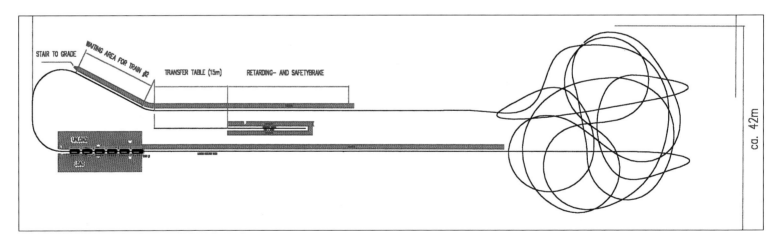

who wouldn't be caught dead riding a coaster will recognize the chain lift's rhythmic *changka-changka-changka* incantation as it drags cars skyward. For decades, that slow climb to the first summit was a mandatory part of the voyage. But these days, the chain lift is now in the optional-parts bin.

In the late 1970s, German designer Anton Schwarzkopf introduced his compact shuttle loop coasters, rides that use flywheel-powered push-carts to hurl trains down a long straightaway. Riders would soar through a single vertical loop and climb a nearly 90-degree spire, where they'd peak

Left: This psychotic hodgepodge of steel is Six Flags Fiesta Texas's *Poltergiest*, an unenclosed version of a Premier Rides continuous-circuit LIM coaster. See if you can figure out just how a train makes its way through that mess; it's not easy.

Below: One of the original Anton Schwarzkopf–designed, catapult-propelled shuttle coasters still on active duty is *Montezooma's Revenge*, which opened in 1978. Riders are mechanically yanked down a straightaway to a top speed of 55 miles per hour (88.5kph) to race through a single vertical loop and climb a steep spire.

and fall right back down, traveling through the short course in reverse. After racing back through the station, the train would climb a second spire and return to a final stop (Knott's Berry Farm's *Montezooma's Revenge* and Six Flags AstroWorld's *Greezed Lightnin'* are two operating examples of these high-intensity devices). But Schwarzkopf's shuttle coasters were just the beginning of his gifts to the coaster community.

In 1996, Paramount's Kings Island and Kings Dominion concurrently debuted a pair of roller coasters called *Outer Limits: Flight of Fear* (the *Outer Limits* prefix was recently dropped; they're both now just *Flight of Fear*). These identical, fully enclosed attractions introduced the world to the brutal intensity of the linear induction motor (LIM) roller coaster. Conceived by Premier Rides (in conjunction with Force Engineering, a company that

manufactures LIMs for the transportation industry), the two *Flight of Fear*s made history by dispensing with standard chain lifts and relying instead on massive doses of electromagnetic energy to thrust 7-ton (6.5t) trains from 0 to 55 miles per hour (88.5kph) in less than four seconds. The coasters further disoriented riders by flinging them through a massive steel "spaghetti bowl" of twisting rails, incorporating twenty-five horizontal curves, thirty vertical curves, and four loop-de-loop inversions. The development of these attractions was so revolutionary that Premier Rides earned two industry awards for its efforts: Technology Applied to Amusements, and Major Theme/Amusement Park Ride/Attraction.

Induction motors are less esoteric than you might expect. If your household appliances include a garbage disposal, hair dryer, or furnace fan, you've got something that utilizes an induction motor within arm's reach. Of course, those little puppies are rotary induction motors, creating—you guessed it—rotary motion. An alternating current is fed into a donut-shaped electrical coil called a stator. Located concentrically inside the stator coil is a circular ring of metal bars called the rotor. As an alternating current throbs through the stator coil, an electromagnetic field is created that spins the rotor and anything that happens to be attached to it.

To create linear motion, one simply unrolls the stator coil into a flat strip and passes a metal sheet through the resulting electromagnetic field to get straight-line acceleration. On Premier's LIM coaster trains, a conductive aluminum fin extends horizontally off either side of each car, below the seats and above the wheelbase. The stator coils are rigged to sandwich the fins from above and below, all the way down the launch track. Each pair of coils, which typically number in the hundreds, is

powered up in sequence, rapidly pulling the train from rest to its maximum velocity.

In the few years since *Flight of Fear* knocked our socks off, Premier Rides has continued to build LIM-powered beasts for parks around the world. There's *Mad Cobra* at Japan's Suzuka Circuitland, two identical *Mr. Freeze* coasters at Six Flags St. Louis and Six Flags Over Texas, *Poltergeist* at Six Flags Fiesta Texas, *The Joker's Jinx* at Six Flags America, and *Speed: The Ride* at the Sahara Hotel and Casino in Las Vegas.

Below: Riders aboard *Mad Cobra* (Japan's Suzuka Circuitland), the only LIM coaster in the Land of the Rising Sun, curl through just one of this coaster's innumerable track twists.

Opposite: Seen clearly in this shot of Six Flags Over Texas' *Mr. Freeze* are the train's horizontal fins. These metal "wings" are what the coaster's linear induction motors grab with electro-magnetic force, propelling the train into action.

Premier Rides

Three words, friends: linear induction motors.

Premier's initial projects, the enclosed *Runaway Mountain* "compact coaster" for Six Flags Over Texas and the 330-foot- (100.5m) tall Observation Tower for Six Flags Elitch Gardens, were hardly the stuff of legend. But in 1996, this company blew us away with a pair of enclosed roller coasters that set a new standard for high-velocity thrills: the *Flight of Fear* coasters at Paramount's Kings Island and Kings Dominion. Harnessing the explosive power of LIMs, the two *Flight of Fear* coasters literally pushed scream machines into a brave new world of high-tech horror.

The company's LIM coaster portfolio now includes *Mad Cobra* at Japan's Suzuka Circuitland, *Poltergeist* at Six Flags Fiesta Texas, and *The Joker's Jinx* at Six Flags America, three rides that are almost identical in layout to the *Flight of Fear* twins yet are not enclosed. Premier has also developed several linear induction shuttle coasters like the two *Mr. Freeze* coasters at Six Flags St. Louis and Six Flags Over Texas and *Speed: The Ride* at the Sahara Hotel and Casino in Las Vegas, all three of which feature vertical spires more than 200 feet (61m) tall. Last but not least, there's Six Flags Great Adventure's *Batman & Robin: The Chiller*, the world's only side-by-side LIM shuttle twosome.

More recently, Premier has begun marketing flume ride/roller coaster hybrids they call liquid coasters. The first of these amphibious contraptions, dubbed *Buzzsaw Falls*, opened at Missouri's Silver Dollar City in 1999, and in 2001 Finland's Linnanmaki Amusement Park got its own *Vonkaputous*, or "Speed Fall."

Premier is committed to remaining a force in "extreme" coaster innovation. Here's a fact that speaks volumes about Premier Rides: Jim Seay, the company's owner and president, once worked for Hughes Aircraft as an aerospace engineer. Enough said.

Batman & Robin: The Chiller

Only at Six Flags Great Adventure will you find a side-by-side pair of LIM coasters, *Batman & Robin: The Chiller*. This dynamic duo improved upon Premier Rides' award-winning *Flight of Fear* coasters in three ways: there are two different courses, each blessed with uniquely devious pleasures; riders travel through the wild trackwork both forward and backward; and both coasters are even faster.

Pity poor Gotham City: once again, this fine metropolis is in the crippling grip of a major crime wave, thanks to the subzero psychosis of Mr. Freeze's evildoings. The Ice Man has set up shop in his elaborately sinister Freeze Generator and neighboring Observatory, and it's up to us to help the Caped Crusader enter the hideout and put an end to his wicked deeds.

Up to the challenge?

Below: Seen from this angle, the distinctions between *Batman & Robin: The Chiller's* two courses are crystal clear. The blue Batman track features a 139-foot- (42.5m) tall vertical U-turn, sometimes referred to as a "top hat" inversion, while the red Robin track doubles the fun with a 105-foot- (32m) tall cobra roll. Then both tracks meet to pirouette through side-by-side barrel rolls on the way up 200-foot- (61m) tall ramps.

Before you answer, take a good look at what awaits: stroll over to the Movietown section of the park; facing the queue, you can eyeball the entire length of the ride. To your left, the 200-foot- (61m) high incline jutting into the heavens above the Freeze Generator is plenty interesting to look at. But turn your head to the right, moving your gaze past the inclined heartline inversions, past the horizontal launch rail, past the Observatory, and you find yourself staring at the tower. This comic book—bright blue and red latticework of steel is enough to leave you agog.

The blue Batman track makes a vertical climb and inverts at the peak of the tower to dive straight back down toward the ground. The red Robin track curls up into an inversion, whips around to the right, and pours back into another inversion, also heading back for terra firma. Here's when folks either mutter a firm "No, thank you" and walk away or make a frantic dash for the entrance.

HOT WHEELS ON STEEL COASTERS

Left: In this image of the blue Batman train, we can see the complex wheel systems that keep the train securely locked to the rails (which, by the way, are standard on just about every roller coaster in existence). There are the road wheels that roll on top of the rail, the side-friction wheels that extend horizontally off the outside of the rails, and the upstop wheels that run beneath the rails.

Standing in line, you'll be able to take in a launch or two before you enter the darkness of the Freeze Generator. First, there are three loud industrial blasts from an air horn (like you hear before they set off dynamite at a construction site), then a muffled BANG! and the instant screaming that only an LIM launch can create. If you don't blink, you can catch a train rocketing out of the Freeze Generator; see how every skull is plastered back against the headrests? The train rips through the Observatory and makes its way up onto the tower. After completing the multidirectional nastiness there, the cars roar back behind the Observatory and up onto the incline, twist through the heartline inversion, and climb up to the peak. Just when it looks like gravity will drag the train to a halt, another string of LIMs takes hold and pulls the train right up to the tippy-top of that 200-foot-

(61m) high ramp. Then the train falls backward. More screaming.

Before you enter the Freezemeister's frigid den, the line splits in two. On your right, the Batman track takes you higher in the tower and provides that delectable 90-degree plunge. To the left, the Robin track offers an extra inversion and more disorientation.

The two lines snake independently through the brick-walled hallways of the Freeze Generator and then meet again on opposite sides of the dimly lit Launch Room. Inside the confines of this chamber, the full sonic assault of each launch is enough to cover your flesh with goose pimples. There's an amplified countdown, the three loud air horn blasts, a low hum as the LIMs juice up, and that righteous BANG! as the trains are released. Oh, and of course, all that wild screaming—are there any sounds sweeter?

Right: Six Flags Great Adventure's *Batman & Robin: The Chiller* presents a handsome profile. To the left is the inversion-packed tower, with Batman's 139-foot- (42.5m) tall vertical inversion and Robin's 105-foot- (32m) tall cobra roll. To the right are the parallel 200-foot- (61m) tall inclines where trains rise, come to a stop, and fall back down to run the entire course again backward.

The low-slung trains are dressed in the same vivid blue and red tones of the tracks. If you choose to go for the front seat, you'll be pleased to note that the nose of the forward car is short and unobtrusive; the view down the straightaway is blissfully unimpeded.

After the restraints are locked firmly into position, there's a few final seconds to prepare for the heart-racing ordeal that awaits—just enough time to squirm around in our seats and share a panicked giggle with the fellow lunatics sitting in the car next to us. Suddenly, the shrill blast of the air horn signals the imminent launch.

Three...The countdown starts, and we whip around to face forward, gripping the restraints with white-knuckled panic.

Two...We can feel the tracks coming alive with power, the electricity flowing into those humming LIMs.

One...We are still motionless and most of the train is already screaming ... BANG!

No matter how many times we've done it, each LIM launch is as terrifying as the last. That explosive acceleration is a horrible treat, our inner child alternately hollering "Please make it stop!" and "Faster, faster!" We're outside the Freeze

Generator, through the Observatory, and at the base of the tower, traveling at 65 miles per hour (104.5kph), in just four seconds.

The Robin train immediately soars up and into its first inversion, 105 feet (32m) above the ground. The cars peel up and over, twist to the right, dive, and then twist to the right once more, entering the second inversion, again flipping over at 105 feet (32m) high. Down we plunge to the base of the tower, heading back toward the Freeze Generator. Delicious.

The Batman train starts heading skyward and keeps on going, straight up, to 139 feet (42.5m).

Up and over, the train makes a vertical U-turn, and now we're poised to drop back down, facing a nice, long 90-degree fall. As we sit in the front seat, this moment is a rare thrill indeed. That rush as we plummet straight down like a dive-bomber—there are few pleasures experienced while fully clothed that are finer than this, friends.

Once through the maelstrom of the tower's trackwork, both courses run parallel up the incline. We hurtle past the Observatory and into a 45-degree-angle heartline inversion. The trains continue up the long ramp, gradually slowing—but before we begin to slide backward, we can feel the

electromagnetic pull of another array of LIMs and the trains climb even higher, nearly to the peak of the 200-foot- (61m) high structure. A pause, and the motors let go.

The journey facing forward was unnerving, but to do it all over again backwards—dropping, flipping, wrenching from side to side, scrambling straight up and then plunging straight down, without any way to anticipate what's coming next....

Back in the station, when we step away from the train, we feel no shame though we need help walking down the exit corridor. Weak-kneed and dizzy is the way we're supposed to feel.

Though just single-track models with fewer inversions than *The Chiller*, Premier's two *Mr. Freeze* coasters in Texas and Missouri are equally gut-busting. After a 0-to-70-mph (112.5kph) launch, the trains make a 150-foot- (46m) high vertical U-turn and fall straight back down to sweep through an elevated, highly banked curve and climb a relentlessly vertical 236-foot (72m) tower. Once electromagnetically pulled up to an altitude above 200 feet (61m) and dropped, they also scramble back through their courses in reverse.

Although Premier was the first, it is no longer the sole provider of such rocket sled–like devices; more and more manufacturers are getting into the act with their own take on nongravitational propulsion. Bolliger & Mabillard's *Incredible Hulk* coaster at Islands of Adventure works miracles with an inclined spinning-tire launch system. Vekoma engineered the linear synchronous motor–launched *Rock 'n' Roller Coaster* for the Disney-MGM Studios park and *Superman: The Ride* at Six Flags Holland. Finally, there's Intamin's *Volcano: The Blast Coaster* at Kings Dominion, the world's fastest and only continuous-circuit linear induction-powered *inverted* coaster. Ready for blastoff?

Opposite: At Six Flags Over Texas, the LIM-powered *Mr. Freeze* shuttle coaster reaches the midpoint of its journey, a 218-foot- (66.4m) tall spike. There, linear induction motors lift the train high and then release it, forcing riders to endure the entire course all over again, backwards.

Left: After its spinning-tire launch and somersault through a zero-G roll, Islands of Adventure's *Incredible Hulk* coaster dives down and powers through a colossal cobra roll over the park's central lake.

Volcano: The Blast Coaster

In 1979, Kings Dominion added a huge artificial mountain at the back end of the park and packed it with three attractions. Hidden behind the craggy walls of The Lost World, thrill seekers could sample *Atlantis*, a flume ride; *The Mine Train*, a journey into the mountain's dark recesses; and *Timeshaft*, a themed stick-you-to-the-walls rotor. Each of these rides was pleasantly diverting and the ominous mountain looked pretty keen, but The Lost World promised more excitement than it delivered. Attractions came and went, and after a spell, The Lost World went silent. Like a time bomb ticking away, this dormant mountain was waiting to explode.

Now owned by Paramount Parks, Kings Dominion's planners were ready to create a ride that would let this dramatic structure live up to its potential. In conjunction with the renowned thrill-ride designers at Intamin, AG, the Paramount Parks Design and Entertainment group envisioned a scream machine that would become a truly precedent-setting attraction. It would be the world's first inverted LIM-launched roller coaster, with a 155-foot (47m) vertical climb straight up and out the very peak of the mountain. But no one had ever strapped LIMs onto an inverted coaster track, and there had never been an inverted ride with a completely vertical launch. "Ambitious" didn't even begin to describe it. To no one's surprise, there were delays, but after months of adjustments Intamin pulled it off. On August 3, 1998, *Volcano: The Blast Coaster* officially erupted with white-hot fury....

Unlike other electromagnetically launched coasters, *Volcano* does not immediately surge forward, rocketing us into never-never land. No, the tension builds gradually as the train slowly floats through a 90-degree bend to the left, positioning us before a long, black tunnel through the Lost World's mountain. Girding our loins, anticipating that moment when the juice will cut loose, we creep away from the comforts of the warm sun over a murky pool of water. Any second now.

Then we hear a glorious sound—that fine whine of impeccable vintage, the ascending squeal of invisible forces thrusting the train to what feels like Mach 1 in just seconds. Faster and faster, we cut through the air, the seats pushing against our backs with merciless strength. Smooth and constant, the acceleration is beyond any other inverted coaster—and it's only the first big push we're gonna get.

The train blasts back into daylight as we exit the mountain and surge to the left. The track banks hard and fast, tossing us away from the ground, and we begin to race through a massive horizontal curve. Off the starboard side, the *Flight of Fear* building is reduced to a blur. We're traveling at awesome speed, near 70 miles per hour (112.5kph), charging along like an F-16; though the train has yet to really change altitude, our spirits are already flying high. The track levels off as we enter a straightaway right back into the mountain— and now the fireworks really begin.

Like a set of afterburners, the second array of LIMs pours it on and we reenter the mountain, ready to go up and out. Inside the pitch-black core, locked down into jet-propelled La-Z-Boys, we feel ourselves tilting way back until we're completely reclined. Through a dense mist, our vehicle performs a completely unnatural act, plowing straight up a vertical section of track. There's a slight twist to the left and once more we're blinded by the sun's rays—except now we have to tilt our heads down to see that big ball of light. We're upside-down for the first time, curling over the lip of the crater, spewing out the top of this volcano 155 feet (47m) above the ground. Boys and girls, we can put this one on the list of Greatest Thrill-Seeking Moments.

We whip back around and head to the left, making a banked turn around the peak and toward the front of the mountain. Keep in mind that we're still

Below: *Volcano: The Blast Coaster* tosses its riders through one of three elevated barrel rolls outside the attraction's man-made mountain. Engineered by Intamin, this scream machine is not only among the world's fastest inverted roller coasters, it's also the world's only continuous-circuit, inverted, LIM-powered coaster.

Right: After years of research, Vekoma introduced the world's first "flying" coaster at Paramount's Great America in 2000. Under the moniker *Stealth*, this mega-high-tech ride holds its passengers completely prone and hanging beneath the rails as it soars through one inversion after another.

more than 100 feet (30.5m) in the sky. Nice view up here, isn't it? It's about to get nicer. We enter the first barrel roll and the world turns upside down at a very...very...leisurely...clip. Keys, wallets, and spare change all threaten to spill free; loose clothing rides up our bodies.

Finishing the barrel roll, we swing around another wide, 180-degree bend, with barrel roll number two dead ahead. Again, as we fly up and over, personal belongings threaten to take flight. We scrape past the mountain's surface, navigate a turn to the right, and head back behind the big rock, where barrel roll number three is tucked away. After a twisting 80-foot (24.5m) dive, we burrow back into the mountain, where the brakes grab hold and quickly bring us to a stop.

Flying Coasters

From the moment our earliest ancestors first looked up at birds winging through the blue yonder, we can be sure they were thinking, "Gee, that looks like fun. Wish I could do that." Nowadays, thanks to Orville and Wilbur Wright, who finally defied the naysayers in 1903, powered flight is commonplace. But that almost primal urge to soar freely through the skies is still spawning technological progress.

In 1987 designers at Vekoma began dreaming about a roller coaster that would mimic the sensation of flight. Years passed without much progress, but in 1992, a brainstorming session produced the first artist's renderings of what would be called the Flying Dutchman, and engineering work shifted into higher gear. By 1996, potential solutions to several major hurdles had been identified, including how to load passengers, harness them in, and rotate them into a prone, face-down position. Vekoma then approached Paramount Parks with an offer: would Paramount be interested in codeveloping the Flying Dutchman?

In December 1996, representatives from Vekoma, Paramount Parks, and the TNO Center for Human Factors (the Netherlands' answer to NASA) met with Dr. Richard Brown, the leading biodynamicist in the amusement industry, to begin feasibility studies. What followed were two solid years of research involving the big brains from a wide-ranging collection of academic and commercial engineering outfits, among them NLR, the Dutch Institute for Aerospace and Space Travel; the Aerospace Department of Delft University; Schroth Systems GmbH, fabricators of harnesses for Formula One race cars, power boats, and high-performance aircraft; and Stork RMO, a Dutch company that engineers high-speed railway trains. Proprietary software was employed to analyze every aspect of the ride system, from the track and train configuration to the passenger-restraint ergonomics. Real-world G-force tests were conducted with the same centrifuges used to examine the physiological effects on fighter pilots and astronauts. By the end of 1998, Vekoma had begun "swing tests" of the preliminary harness mechanism. It was time to begin full-scale construction.

Stealth

Typically, a prototype attraction is built at the factory; only when the concept is proven viable does it move into public view. Not in the case of the Flying Dutchman—Paramount and Vekoma chose to build the actual prototype right on the property of Paramount's Great America in Santa Clara, California, and coaster enthusiasts around the world watched it come together with spirited expectations. By mid-spring 1999, with the coaster's primary structure complete, the park was compelled to announce that *Stealth*, the world's first flying coaster, would open in 2000.

From July through October 1999 the ride system was put through its paces, and as with any prototype, modifications were made. First, the original upper-body restraint, a rigid over-the-shoulder harness, was replaced with more pliant, padded belt-and-buckle gear (courtesy of Schroth Systems

Below: Though *Stealth* offers all manner of heart-pounding inversions, one appreciates this flying coaster's idiosyncratic pleasures most when just soaring along, face down, arms spread wide, and free as a bird.

GmbH). Second, the individual cars would not tilt back into "flight" position while moving up the lift hill, as was first proposed. Instead, engineers were able to dispense with complicated onboard mechanicals by fully reclining the vehicles right in the station.

Over the winter, the track and supports received their final coats of paint, the station was completed, and the last few bolts and screws were tightened. At long last, the greatly anticipated $17 million *Stealth* was cleared for takeoff.

At first glance, *Stealth* might not blow your synapses; after all, vertical loops, corkscrews, and 115-foot (35m) lift hills are a dime a dozen these days. But when a train goes into action, you'll start to appreciate what you're about to experience.

Even more pulse-racing (or disturbing, depending on your eagerness to board) is watching the preflight procedure. Four per row, passengers settle into the fighter-jet gray bucket seats and squirm into those heavy-duty chest harnesses, buckles snapping tight. A lower-body restraint, with padded calf supports, rises up between each pair of legs. And when all are secure, the cars tip back all the way until the entire trainload is lying flat, staring up at the heavens. If you think it looks freaky, wait until you feel it happen....

First, there's the chest harness. When the ride operator cinches it good and tight around our rib cages, we're jolted into realizing how important that harness will be for the next two minutes of our lives. And when leg supports lock down the lower half of our bodies, we feel less like passengers and more like test pilots.

In one smooth motion, the seats flip backward. Blood rushes into our heads. All we can see is sky. The train begins to move. Stitched onto the front of each chest harness are two looped yellow straps, the only thing we can grab hold of—and we grab.

We feel the temptation to raise our noggins and look back at the station as we pull away, but it's much more fun, almost surreal, to just gaze straight up, watch the clouds drift by, see two rail sections sweep past overhead, and feel the chain lift engage behind our backs—without any idea of what's coming next.

Suddenly, we're no longer completely reclined— the train has risen up the first 30-degree slope. Because of our captive posture, we simply can't anticipate when we'll reach the apex. Tension mounts as we move higher, waiting for something to happen.

Finally, it does: we slide over the top, our torsos tip back, and *Stealth* picks up airspeed. It's time to pry our fingers out of those straps, spread our arms wide, and get ready to fly.

In the first of four acrobatic 180-degree twists, the train curls completely upside down. Without warning, the sky disappears and gravity pulls us hard against those harnesses. We're left gaping down at the ground more than 100 feet (30.5m) below. Brothers and sisters, this is what it means to be inverted.

Charging forward, the train glides around a turn and we start to plunge headfirst toward the earth, diving like birds of prey. We fight the fear, keep those arms outstretched, and go with the flow.

Our flying machine reaches a maximum cruise velocity of 51 miles per hour (82kph) and pulls back up, zooming into a horseshoe inversion. Up and over we careen, flung to the right and nearly tossed onto our backs again. The sky whips in and out of view in a heartbeat before we scream down a second major descent. By this point we're already smitten, but these first few gentle maneuvers are just warm-ups for the mind-melting gymnastics ahead. From here on in, it's like we're strapped to the underside of a nuclear missile gone completely haywire.

Vekoma Rides Manufacturing

It was way back in 1926 that Vekoma first began bending raw steel into practical mechanical devices. Established in Vlodrop, the Netherlands, the company initially focused on designing and manufacturing not thrill rides, but agricultural and petrochemical equipment. Fortunately for us, Vekoma shifted gears in the 1960s. For some time, Vekoma specialized primarily in roller coasters, both standard models and one-of-a-kind layouts. But in the 1990s, the firm rapidly expanded the list of devices in its inventory—all sorts of spinning, flipping, splashing, twirling, looping, shuddering machines with names like *Para Tower*; *Rapid River*; *Sky Flyer*; *Sky Shuttle*; *Waikiki Wave* and its wilder sibling, the *W.W. Super Flip*; *Swinging Carousel*; *Flash Dance*; and the *Mad House*.

Vekoma is most well known for its stock suspended looping coasters (SLCs), like the *Mind Eraser* at Riverside Six Flags America and Six Flags Elitch Gardens, and their amazingly popular Boomerang shuttle coasters, now found at literally dozens of parks worldwide. In 1997, Vekoma came up with an inverted Boomerang, cleverly dubbed the Invertigo, a machine that's rapidly gaining a notorious reputation (see Paramount's Great America's *Invertigo*, Paramount's Kings Island's *Face/Off*, and Six Flags America's *Two Face: The Flip Side*).

Vekoma has supplied the mechanicals for some of Disney's major coasters, including the indoor, LSM-launched *Rock 'n' Roller Coaster* at Disney-MGM Studios within the company's Florida resort. Vekoma also delivered the aquatic ride system for Universal Studios' *Jurassic Park: The Ride*.

And since garnering adulation with the Flying Dutchman coaster, they've developed their Giant Inverted Boomerang (*Déjà Vu* at Six Flags Magic Mountain, Six Flags Great America, and Six Flags Over Georgia), and the Motorbike Launch coaster, which won the International Association of Amusement Parks and Attraction's "Best New Product Award" in 2004.

As we regain a little altitude we hit a second abrupt track twist and flip over, jamming face-up through a banked curve and rocketing into the base of the vertical loop.

With our craniums leading the way and our spines parallel to the rails, *Stealth* makes navigating an upright 360 a completely unique adventure. Bizarre and brilliant.

We leave the loop behind and tear into another turn, passing over the lift hill and hitting a third 180-degree flip-flop. Face-down once again, we sail toward the outer edge of *Stealth*'s course, with corkscrews off to our right. Before we tackle that horizontal vortex, we've got to get properly oriented. The fourth and final 180-degree track rotation whirls us over, and a-barrel rollin' we go. Once, twice, somersaulting madly, *Stealth* scrambles us like human omelettes. Just as our inner ears are begging for mercy, we slide out of the pandemonium and ease back into the station. In just over

Left: This red-and-blue SLC, called *Mind Eraser*, swings its payload of happy campers at Six Flags Elitch Gardens in Denver, Colorado.

2,780 feet (847m), this flying coaster has put us through up to 4.7 positive Gs and 2.5 negative Gs. That, people, is the Wright stuff.

In 2003, *Stealth* was dismantled and shipped to Paramount's Carowinds in Charlotte, North Carolina, where it's now in operation as the creepy *BORG Assimilator*. And it remains only one of three Vekoma flyers in the U.S., along with Six Flags America's *Batwing* in Maryland and Geauga Lake's *X-Flight* in Ohio. (Those last two swapped out

Stealth's final corkscrews with tighter heartline twists and got bonus final horizontal spirals, too.)

Fortunately, Bolliger & Mabillard have joined the steel coaster "air corps" with their own twist on the flying coaster. Since the debut of *AIR* at England's Alton Towers in 2002, B&M has delivered a trio of rides called *Superman: Ultimate Flight* to Six Flags Over Georgia, New Jersey's Six Flags Great Adventure, and Illinois' Six Flags Great America, and more are sure to follow.

EXTREME MACHINES

CHAPTER 4

There are scream machines and then there are extreme machines—supersized, rocket-fueled roller coasters that show no pity for the meek. Wood or steel, out-and-back or twister, no matter what their configuration, all of them have this cautionary message for the thrill seeker wannabe: "If you can't run with the big dogs, *stay on the porch.*"

Hypercoasters

A little more than ten years ago, a new term entered the thrill-ride lexicon. Cedar Point, once home to one of the first *Switchback Railways*, was instrumental in the development of what are now known as "hypercoasters," any coaster with a hill or drop measuring more than 200 feet (61m) in height. On May 6, 1989, a key date in roller coaster history, the Arrow Dynamics–designed $8 million *Magnum XL-200* was officially opened at Cedar Point.

Richard Kinzel, the president and CEO of Cedar Fair, L.P., owners of Cedar Point, explained the *Magnum XL-200*'s genesis: "Cedar Point has one of the oldest roller coaster heritages in the world. Our first roller coaster, the 25-foot- [7.5m] tall *Switchback Railway*, opened in 1892 and traveled at 10 miles per hour [16kph]. Thrill rides are our birthright, and we needed a signature attraction that would make a statement. At the time, the industry was really into looping roller coasters, but I wanted something different, completely one of a kind. It had to be the tallest and fastest steel thriller in the world, but feature the hills and turns experienced on classic wooden roller coasters like the Coney Island *Cyclone*."

In August 1988, site preparation and construction began. More than forty companies spent ten months battling Mother Nature's wintry fury to set more than 350 concrete footers in place (some with bases larger than a city bus) and weld together 568 tons (515t) of 10-foot- (30.5m) wide steel columns. Hauled by a 1,060-foot- (323m) long, 7-ton (6.3t) lift chain to the top of what was then a record-annihilating 205-foot (62.5m) apex, *Magnum XL-200*'s inaugural train rocketed into our hearts at a speed of 72 miles per hour (116kph). Its first 60-degree, 194-foot- (59m) tall descent was the preamble to a 5,106-foot- (1,556m) long airtime blitzkrieg, earning the coaster instant adulation.

Soon after *Magnum*'s blow-the-roof-off initiation, Arrow Dynamics went on to build Kennywood's *Steel Phantom*, an 80-mph (129kph) looping hypercoaster whose second drop—its largest—fell 225 feet (68.5m); Buffalo Bill's *Desperado* on the California/Nevada border; and Blackpool Pleasure Beach's *Pepsi Max Big One* in England. But Arrow wouldn't remain the only hypercoaster purveyor for long. D.H. Morgan Manufacturing, Inc., first

Left: Feast your eyes on what was once the tallest, longest, and fastest continuous-circuit roller coaster in the world: Nagashima Spa Land's *Steel Dragon 2000*. Though it no longer holds either the speed or height record—not by a long shot—it may be some time before anyone builds an unthemed coaster more expensive than the *Dragon*—this vast mountain range of metal set back its owners a cool $51 million.

gained entry to the hypercoaster club in 1996 with *Wild Thing* at Minnesota's Valleyfair! theme park. Standing 207 feet (63m) tall, with a top speed of 74 miles per hour (119kph), *Wild Thing* made Morgan a force to be reckoned with. One year later, Pennsylvania's Dorney Park took delivery of a Morgan hypercoaster that is still considered one of the most exciting steel roller coasters in existence.

Steel Force

In 1860, Solomon Dorney opened a fish hatchery along Pennsylvania's Cedar Creek, complete with several trout ponds for the neighborhood anglers. His humble Fish Weir quickly became popular and Dorney began to plan a bigger future for this piece of real estate. He added games, a small zoo, refreshment stands, a hotel and restaurant, and, yes, some mechanical rides. By 1884, Solomon had built a bona fide amusement park, which he renamed Dorney's Trout Ponds and Summer Resort.

By the turn of the century, the Allentown-Kutztown Traction Company, the owners of the local trolley line, purchased the park from Dorney and brought in some concessionaires. Jacob Plarr, an enterprising Philadelphian, contributed a Dentzel carousel and Dorney Park really took off.

The year 1923 was a milestone: Dorney got its first coaster, the imaginatively named *Coaster*, and there was no turning back. Solomon, in his wisdom, had laid the groundwork for some serious thrillmongering, and today, Dorney's former trout ponds are home to another of America's elite hypercoasters, the 200-foot- (61m) tall *Steel Force*.

In these heady days of cobra rolls, linear induction motors, and flying coasters, there is something romantically pure about your basic out-and-back, upright-sitting, loop-free coaster. Don't get me wrong—*Steel Force* is as masterfully engineered as

any other coaster. It's just that this ride's mission, like *Magnum*'s before it, is wonderfully straightforward: carry us to an insane height, let us go, and get our rears flying out of our seats as many times as possible. As a matter of fact, *Steel Force* provides so much airtime that you'll wonder why they didn't call it *Air Force*. And if you're looking for maximum airtime, you know where to head: the backseat, the tail of the whip, the place where evil dwells....

The brakes are released and we roll toward destiny. After a jog to the left, we begin to climb that mountain of metal. Off to our right sits the entire park; on our left is the pond that Solomon Dorney first dipped his toes in. Before we know it, we're teetering on the edge of a 205-foot (62.5m) plunge.

As the cars begin to fall forward, the screams rise from our throats instinctively. Within seconds, we're diving down at 75 miles per hour (120.5kph) directly into a 120-foot- (36.5m) long tunnel. Speed—raw, powerful speed...there's nothing like it. We can't help but appreciate the reverberating roar of the train as it plows through that tunnel: aural bliss.

Blasting back into daylight, we race up onto the second hill, this one a still-staggering 161 feet (49m) high. Back down and then up and into the approach to the *Force*'s awesome far-end spiral. We've traveled all the way over to *Hercules*, Dorney's former coaster king, and now it's time to head back. Before we do, there's some high-G pleasures to be had in the form of a massive 360-degree turnaround. We feel our necks straining to hold our heads upright as the coaster banks and turns, turns, turns, shrieking like a bat out of hell.

We bolt toward the left again, and here's where things get nice and goofy. We haul up onto a flat, straight section of track that seems to hold some kind of brake run. If there are brakes at work, they take care of business without much damage to our

Right: Like *Apollo's Chariot*, Six Flags Great America's *Raging Bull* (pictured) is a Bolliger & Mabillard "Speed" hypercoaster. But this particular model is a twister, with more banking turns.

Opposite: Bolliger & Mabillard's first hypercoaster, Busch Gardens Williamsburg's *Apollo's Chariot*, falls from the sky to reach a top speed of 73 miles per hour (117.5kph). The out-and-back coaster's "Speed" trains, elevated seats without any front or side walls, maximize the impact of that first 210-foot (64.0m) descent.

forward-moving progress. But it's a long stretch, so we can catch our breath and we wonder when things are going to—

WHAM! We're not in the front seat and can't see it coming, so there's no way to prepare for the sudden, furious dive off the brake run. We're thrown up against the lap bar and held there as the train hustles down. Up and over, and we're out of our seat again. Back down and into another tunnel, right alongside the base of the first drop...and up again...and down and up and down and up, flying over hills one right after another, our hindquarters spending more time out of the seats than in them. Mechanical bulls wish they could throw us around like this.

After one final little hump, we cruise over the queue, slow to a crawl, and glide into the station. If all that doesn't make us smile, nothing will.

Morgan Manufacturing completed its 1990s hypercoaster trilogy in 1998 with *Mamba*, another 205-foot- (62.5m) tall triumph, for Missouri's Worlds of Fun. For its 2001 season, Kennywood hired Morgan to revamp the venerable *Steel Phantom*. That coaster's signature hyperdive was extended by 5 feet (1.5m), maxing out at 230 feet (70m), and its four looping inversions were replaced with more drops, sweeping turns, and a plethora of bunny hops, creating what is now known as *Phantom's Revenge*.

Nitro

In 2001, Bolliger & Mabillard pushed us even closer to the ozone layer with the tallest roller coaster they'd ever devised, Six Flags Great Adventure's notorious *Nitro*, a 230-foot- (70m) tall, 5,394-foot- (1,644m) long speed freak that attains a maximum velocity of nearly 80 miles per hour (129kph). Those who had experienced B&M's earlier

hypercoaster feats in 1999 with *Raging Bull* in Six Flags Great America and *Apollo's Chariot* in Busch Gardens Williamsburg were familiar with their "Speed" trains' radically minimalist restraints and frontless, sideless cars with elevated seats. As soon as riders would hop into the molded posterior cradles, their feet would be swaying freely high above the floor of the car, and the only thing that would hold them down would be a clamshell-shaped lap bar—no upper-body harnesses and nothing to obscure the view of the port and starboard sides. *Apollo's Chariot*'s vertical falls add up to an awesome total of 825 feet (251.5m), surpassing every other roller coaster assembled before it. From its first 210-foot (64m), 73-mph (117.5kph) descent to its final ravaging lunge into an excavated 49-foot- (15m) deep ditch, *Apollo's Chariot* is an airtime addict's dream come true. And though *Nitro*'s L-shaped out-and-back layout borrows plenty from *Apollo's Chariot*, this cunning monster has some new tricks up its sleeve....

The entrance to the queue has us looking right at that 230-foot (70m) hill rising up and away in the distance, and what a sight for sore eyes it is. Nothing fancy-schmancy about the rest of the pre-board experience—just a generic switchback stroll to an elevated sheet metal loading dock. But once we're up the stairs and on the platform, waiting for the next train to arrive, we're not thinking about the dearth of visual niceties.

We take the best seat in the house: front row, outer left. Snuggled into those bucket seats, clamshell lap bars locked down, we're off. The train pours right into a nimble, swooping U-turn and rises to engage the chain.

Not quite frozen with terrified anticipation, we look over our shoulders and enjoy a gorgeous bird's-eye view of the entire park. When we look to the

Below: Bolliger & Mabillard's most inversion-crammed coaster is *Dragon Kahn*, at Universal Studios Port Aventura in Spain, with eight upside-down elements from start to finish: a vertical loop, a diving loop, a heartline roll, a cobra roll (with two inversions), another vertical loop, and two corkscrews.

Bolliger & Mabillard

Walter Bolliger and Claude Mabillard, two engineers based in Monthey, Switzerland, are living legends. Most any thrill seeker will agree that their company's name is synonymous with the best in ultramodern steel roller coasters. Bolliger & Mabillard's first effort, the *Iron Wolf* stand-up coaster, built for Chicago, Illinois' Six Flags Great America in 1990, was a stunner; since then, B&M's copious output has just gotten more and more breathtaking. In 1992, the firm took the industry by storm with its patented "no floor inverted" coaster (*Batman—The Ride*, also for Six Flags Great America). *Kumba*, unveiled in 1994 as a "conventional" sit-down, multilooping masterpiece at Busch Gardens Tampa, redefined that genre of scream machines. In England, Alton Towers debuted B&M's Diving Machine, a full-circuit coaster with a nearly 90-degree drop, appropriately called *Oblivion*. In Spain, Universal Studio's Port Aventura showcases B&M's *Dragon Kahn*, a ride that until 1998 was the only eight-inversion roller coaster on the planet.

In the past few years, B&M has continued to defy convention with their audacious floorless coasters (*Hydra: The Revenge* at Dorney Park), their deliriously satisfying speed hypercoasters (*Silver Star* at Europa Park in Germany), their first-class flying coasters (*Superman: Ultimate Flight* at Six Flags Great Adventure), and their daunting Diving Machine (*SheiKra* at Busch Gardens Tampa).

With such amazing ingenuity, it's certain that Bolliger & Mabillard isn't through taking coasters where they've never been before.

right, we see signs that indicate our progressive climb beyond the heights of several famous monuments: the Sphinx, Niagara Falls, the Leaning Tower of Pisa. Soon our attention is drawn to what's off to the left: *Nitro*'s 1-mile- (1.6kph) long riot through the lakeside wilderness. Then we're at the pinnacle.

Up and over, the nose of the train drops. And drops. And drops some more. At 66 degrees, the angle of the first descent is far from completely vertical, but from this dizzying crest, it sure feels like it could be. We raise our arms, extend our legs, and lean forward.

Nitro drops like a bomb. We run amok down into a steel gorge, a torrent of air blasting harder and harder against us while we plummet 215 feet (65.5m) like we were Acapulco cliff divers on our way to the mother of all belly flops.

Bottoming out at a scorching velocity, we storm right back up to the top of a 189-foot (57.5m) peak, and it's at this mesmerizing moment that we most appreciate the front left seat. With negative Gs giving us an upward boost, the train turns and pitches way over to the port side. We look to our left: all that's between us and the cold, bare earth more than eighteen stories below is a whole lot of nothing. And all that's keeping us from getting dumped into the void is that lap restraint.

There's only a mere heartbeat during which to relish this near-death experience, and then *Nitro* charges on, skimming the deck and attacking a 161-foot- (49m) tall camelback hill with full-throttle ferocity. We're airborne again as we soar through the sky and plunge back down.

Then it's hammer time.

At the far end of *Nitro*'s course, we encounter what B&M calls the Hammer Head, a rising, banking, sweeping, diving maneuver that would make a fighter pilot proud. The train rockets up, arcs and

whips to the right, and slams through a complete 180-degree inclined twist at breakneck speed. We like all these positive Gs, but we're in luck because this is just the appetizer.

Shrieking down the outer leg of the Hammer Head, we're prepped for some more airtime, rushing toward another major camelback. High and low we go, rump flotation galore, gearing up for yet another of notorious *Nitro*'s unique delights: its spine-compressing spiral.

Our cars careen through one more tip-us-over turn and surge into the base of this steel vortex. Round and round we go as the whirlpool gets tighter and tighter, the track banks steeper and steeper, the support poles get closer and closer, the positive Gs press down *relentlessly*...and just before our rib cages implode, we zip out of the top of the spiral and cruise over the block brake.

This wouldn't be a proper out-and-backer without a climactic scramble over some pummeling bunny hops, and *Nitro* delivers in spades. We dart off the block-brake stretch and bound over wave after

Below: The 230-foot-(70m) tall *Nitro*, at New Jersey's Six Flags Great Adventure, is one of the latest hyper-coasters from our friends at Bolliger & Mabillard. Like its predecessors, Busch Gardens Williamsburg's *Apollo's Chariot* and Six Flags Great America's *Raging Bull*, Nitro features B&M's sleek, open-air "Speed" trains, seen up close here.

Giovanola

Founded by Joseph Giovanola in 1888, this enterprise based in Monthey, Switzerland, started out as a small metal forging shop. More than a century later, Giovanola Frères SA was a tremendous industrial concern, employing more than three hundred designers, engineers, and factory workers at its 115,000-square-meter plant.

This company was engaged in far more than the assembly of thrill rides. With its gargantuan welding and fabrication equipment, Giovanola had helped construct electrical power stations; water storage tanks and pipelines; highway bridges; driers and filtration systems for the chemical, pharmaceutical, and food industries; and much, much more.

In recent decades Giovanola had also worked behind the scenes to fashion steel into a variety of major roller coasters, free-fall towers, and assorted rides for other companies, including Bolliger & Mabillard and Intamin. In 1998, Giovanola began to directly market itself as a supplier of thrill rides, and the firm burst onto the scene with Six Flags Magic Mountain's *Goliath*, a supercharged hypercoaster, and *Anaconda*, a beautiful inverted coaster for South Africa's Gold Reef City outside Johannesburg. Alas, Giovanola no longer seems to be in business and our world is the worse for it.

undulating yellow steel wave, right up until we simply must come to a stop.

Sure, the back row is terrific, and many will ultimately prefer it, though that unimpeded front-seat view is half of what makes *Nitro* and all of B&M's speed coasters so fabulous. No matter where we end up planting our keisters, we'll make room for this one on our top ten list.

Goliath

The debut American coaster installation from Giovanola, Six Flags Magic Mountain's *Goliath* isn't quite as tall as Japan's *Fujiyama*, a 259-foot- (79m) tall hypertwister with a nearly 230-foot (70m) first drop. But by going subterranean at the base of its principal plunge, *Goliath* trumps *Fujiyama* with a 255-foot (77.5m) descent and a maximum velocity of—drumroll, please—85 miles per hour (136.5kph).

To board this jumbo jet of a scream machine, we dodge between the rock-hewn G-O-L-I-A-T-H letters that stand guard before the entrance to the queue. A switchback trail takes us through what looks to be

the remains of a lost tropical civilization. Swinging around the far end of the boarding station, we climb a tall flight of stairs to where the rubber hits the road. Up on the dock, we get a good look at Giovanola's unique rolling stock. Does that nifty airfoil on the brow of each vehicle perform an aerodynamic function? We're guessing no, but who cares? It looks keen. And the contoured seats with their raised backrests are mighty fine, too. Last among the new details these Giovanola coaches boast is a single yellow lap bar with a funky, indented grab-handle.

Directly out of the station, the train sweeps around a turn and begins climbing. As we rise, we enjoy the thought that we're about to experience one of the tallest and fastest drops on any continuous-circuit roller coaster: 255 feet (77.5m) at an angle of 61 degrees. "Heaven, I'm in heaven"…by the time we hit the pinnacle, we almost *are* in heaven.

The front car tips forward, levels off, and keeps tipping until we can see, more than twenty-four-odd stories down, a black hole in the ground—the entrance to hell.

Left: Its first descent is a whopper, but *Goliath* is about a whole lot more than pure speed. In the background of this shot, beyond its hills, we can see this hypercoaster's mind-boggling assortment of banked turns and spirals, ready to pound riders with positive G-forces.

It's time to put the *Go* in *Goliath*.

Arms up, mouths open, tonsils doing the wacky wiggle, speed pouring on. Speed like there's no tomorrow. Speed so sweet, so raw, we never want to stop falling. Bliss ripples over us, through our hair, into our very being as we scream toward 85 miles per hour (136.5kph).

That wicked little pit comes rushing up, and in a skin-peeling tear, we make like a subway train with Satan at the helm, plowing through the darkness. They say this tunnel is 120 feet (36.5m) long, but it might as well be 120 millimeters, because we're in and out of there *two seconds ago*.

Our five-car fireball shrieks away from damnation and moves on to humiliate what was once the world's tallest woodie, Magic Mountain's *Colossus*. We rise 100 feet (30.5m) above *Colossus*' far turn, leaning over on the right side to look way down at that forlorn pile of lumber.

After that quick turn, we plunge down a second drop that measures up as a hypercoaster descent. We've been lacking airtime, but here it comes. Climbing away from the turf, the train soars over a nice, long gradual hill and we get busy with a few seconds of serious float. We need to enjoy it while it lasts, though, because from here on in our ham shanks aren't going anywhere.

Down off the third hill, we drop, rise, and twist up onto a horizontal stretch alongside the lift hill. Yes, there's a brake and it does a little killjoy duty. We'll be grateful in a minute.

Now we're at the point where positive G-forces come into play. See, this coaster doesn't burn off momentum with a bunch of bunny hops, like the average out-and-back hypermodel. *Goliath* has a completely different game plan; its latter half is nothing but a ton of turns, and that means we're in for a twelve-course feast of positive Gs.

Off the brake run, we curl down a sinuous drop to the left and motor through a tight curve to the right. Feel how our bodies are pressed a little more firmly into the seats? Those G-forces are building.

Out of that turn, we dart beneath some supports, and it's so easy to imagine an earsplitting CLANGCLANGCLANG! as our raised knuckles bash against the green steel. But our eyes don't fool us—we know there's room to spare and if we bring our arms down now, they're staying down.

The train zips up a little ramp and enters *Goliath*'s spiral, a ferocious element that ought to be called the centrifuge: banking, turning, harder and harder…mind fading…body weakening…trying to stay…conscious! This is the real deal, people; some riders report experiencing tunnel vision and near gray-outs. Of those who make the mistake of letting their arms drop during the approach, only the fittest will be able to lift them back up once the train begins to wail around this circular insanity. It is ripsnorting spectacular. We've been warned.

Once we pull out of the centrifuge, there's another set of sweeping curves, though nothing quite so carcass-clobbering—thank goodness.

Finishing it up, we thread back through the spiral and soar back up onto the final brake run.

Positive-G masochists will be overjoyed to learn that Six Flags Over Texas now has its own Giovanola-designed hypercoaster, the equally titanic *Titan*. Its course, while very similar to *Goliath*'s, is even longer, with an extra spiral in the mix. So whether you're in California or the Lone Star State, remember: the centrifuge is waiting for you.

Son of Beast

Steel hypercoasters, once as rare as tanning salons in the Sahara, are well on their way to becoming a healthy worldwide tribe. But there's only one woodie that has managed, so far, to breach the 200-foot (61m) height barrier. That coaster, the world's first hyperwoodie, is Kings Island's *Son of Beast*, the "sequel" to the park's famed *The Beast*.

It took a design and engineering team that included the Roller Coaster Corporation of America, Premier Rides, and the eminent coaster stylist Werner Stengel to devise a ride that upstages *The Beast* with not one but two massive spirals, the first vertical loop on a woodie since the dawn of the twentieth century, and a 214-foot (65m) power dive off a 218-foot (66.5m) lift hill. Its top speed? Seventy-eight miles per hour (125.5kph), about 13 mph (21kph) better than the *The Beast* can muster during normal operation. To call this woodie humongous is a pathetic understatement.

Big Daddy prowls unseen through the impenetrable forest at the back of the park. His spawn, on the other hand, lives large right up front, baring its gnarled teeth and rising up on its hind legs so you can get an eyeful of him from the very first moment you enter Kings Island's Action Zone, just to the left of the park's entrance.

Opposite: Though it held the title for only a few brief months, Six Flags Magic Mountain's *Goliath* was the world's tallest and fastest continuous-circuit roller coaster when it had its official debut on February 10, 2000. Seen here, one of *Goliath*'s trains rips down its signature 255-foot (77.7m) drop, on its way to achieving a maximum velocity of 85 miles per hour (136.8kph).

Left: Though no longer considered colossal in this day and age, Six Flags Magic Mountain's *Colossus* was a gargantuan wooden coaster in its time, leading the way towards ever more monstrous woodies and, eventually, Paramount's Kings Island's *Son of Beast*, the world's first hyperwoodie.

Right: From far overhead, it's even easier to appreciate *Son of Beast*'s commanding presence. The coaster's vertical loop, right in the middle of the course, may look diminutive from this perspective, but it's actually about 118 feet (36m) tall.

As a train climbs up that lumber Mt. Everest, you can hear *Son of Beast* growl, a metallic clatter that seems to carry for miles. Sonny Boy may be many things, but bashful isn't one of them. "You wanna piece of me? I'm right here; come and get me."...

Come and get him we do, in a sunburst yellow and fire-engine red Perimeter Surveillance Vehicle (PSV), the Premier Rides–designed contraption specifically engineered to handle the high-intensity "hard target" pursuit we're about to begin. Our point of departure is Outpost 5, and to get there we've got to stroll up a series of ramps. It may seem odd; they could have built the station far closer to ground level. But the reason they didn't will soon become clear.

As we reach the top of the ascending queue, returning PSVs slide into the station on our left. Very slick, these angular go-mobiles, with their wheel covers, warning stripes, biohazardlike graphics, and, best of all, no over-the-shoulder restraints. Before we board, we look down over the edge of the platform. We are *up there*.

Settling into the seat, we understand why shoulder harnesses aren't necessary—a bulky, wedge-shaped lap bar tucks into our hips for a very secure lockdown. Now it's time to find out if this critter's bite is as bad as his bark.

He sure does start the party with a bang, snarling right down a 51-foot (15.5m) plunge. We think about how many woodies we've ridden that never fall that far...then chew on the fact that this drop is only *one-quarter* the size of what's coming up next, and it makes our fillings tingle.

We swing around to meet the base of the lift. As that chain grabs hold and we begin scaling this southern yellow pine brute, the *Son*'s growl becomes an unholy racket. In every way possible, this coaster is totally aggro.

Right: With its signature loop in the foreground, the only inversion to be found on a wooden coaster anywhere, Paramount's Kings Island's *Son of Beast* carries its victims down a record-destroying 214-foot (65.2m) initial drop.

Finally at the pinnacle, we curl over with the park's Eiffel Tower in the distance. The PSV picks up the pace, rumbling through a righteously unsettling swoop curve—unsettling because this isn't a whisper-quiet, butter-smooth steel coaster maneuver; this is a down and dirty, rock 'em, sock 'em, woodie swoop curve nearly 200 feet (61m) in the sky.

We're up out of the turn and rushing forward—and there it is, a 214-foot- (65m) deep chasm, laminated parallel rails diving at a 55.7-degree angle.

And as the *Son* goes up, so must the *Son* go down.

Roaring like a hellhound, the train flat-out meteors into this timber gorge. We thunder faster and faster, and by the time we're starting to climb back up again, traveling at that 78-mph (125.5kph) velocity, we're thinking it's 178 mph (286.5kph), because this is old-school: loud, mean, and remorseless. The vertical loop blurs by on the left, but we barely register it. Before we know it, we're screaming to the right, getting ready to enter spiral number one.

Seems like we've regained some considerable altitude, yes? We have, brothers and sisters—about 164 feet (50m). Thus entering the spiral means plummeting down America's second-tallest wooden coaster drop. Here's where things start getting seriously hot and heavy.

Ever been in an earthquake? Having spent many years living in southern California, I've gotten a taste of more than a few. The minor ones just shake things up a bit, but the hard-core crust-busters do more than rattle the windows; the ground rhythmically heaves beneath your feet. That closely describes the sensation of exploding through the *Son*'s mammoth spirals. The train doesn't just shiver—it convulses through this magnificently fierce counterclockwise whirlpool. And it lasts a

good, long time, 540 degrees, up and down, around and around, nonstop bestial wrath. Like father, like *Son*, this puppy runs the rings hard.

Once we escape that chaos, there's an amazing moment of grace coming: the loop.

We pull out of the spiral, scoot across a midpoint brake run, make another descent, and then watch the world turn upside down, woodie style.

In any other context, this single vertical inversion would be fairly unremarkable. But in contrast to the agitation we've just endured, the tranquility of this element is a real surprise. With no upper-body confinement, we can spread our arms wide and revel in it all. What a rare treat. Up and over we soar, about 100 feet (30.5m) high…very nice.

Above: Like father, like son: *Son of Beast*'s "Perimeter Surveillance Vehicle" charges around the first of this hyperwoodie's two enormous inclined spirals, both similar to, yet even more aggressive than, *The Beast*'s infamous helix.

Like Bolliger & Mabillard and Giovanola, Intamin is based in Switzerland and has been a force in the industry for several decades. This company does it all: roller coasters (both wood and steel), free-fall towers, water rides, dark rides, monorails, observation towers—you name it, they can build it.

Year after year, Intamin has been involved with a profusion of groundbreaking attractions. In association with Anton Schwarzkopf, Intamin gave the world its first modern vertical loop coaster, the *Great American Revolution*, which opened in 1976 at Magic Mountain in Valencia, California. Intamin also pioneered the development of the free-fall ride and the whitewater-raft ride. Intamin can boast of building one of only two eight-inversion roller coasters in existence: *Monte Makaya* at Brazil's Terra Encantada park (and right now they're working on a coaster that will break that record). Intamin's *Volcano: The Blast Coaster*, at Paramount's Kings Dominion, is the world's only continuous-circuit LIM-launched inverted coaster. And one can't mention Intamin without raising a toast to the company's 100-mph (161kph) Reverse Free Falls, *Tower of Terror* at Australia's Dreamworld and *Superman: The Escape* at Six Flags Magic Mountain, the latter once ranked as the world's tallest and fastest thrill ride.

In 1999 Intamin got hyperactive with Six Flags Darien Lake's *Superman: Ride of Steel*, New York State's first "double-century" dynamo. Sporting a 208-foot (63.5m) lift hill, this coaster soars down a 205-foot (62.5m) slope to fight for truth, justice, and the American way at a top speed of 70 miles per hour (112.5kph)—not quite faster than a speeding bullet, but more than enough to leap over tall buildings in a single bound. In 2000, Intamin whipped up two more *Superman* coasters, one for Six Flags America in Maryland and the other for Six Flags New England in Massachusetts. Six Flags America's superheroic hypercoaster matches the Darien Lake model's 205-foot (62.5m) first drop, but New England's own *Superman*, while still just 208 feet (63.5m) tall, features a primary descent of 221 feet (67.5m). And this particular *Superman*, with a remarkably multifaceted layout, has been praised by many as one of the best steel coasters running. Last but far from least, we can thank Intamin for delivering the world's first giga- *and* strata-coaster.

Opposite: The *Superman: Ride of Steel* hypercoaster at Six Flags New England, like the other Superman rides Intamin has produced, features trains with stadium-style seats: the rear rows in each car are positioned a bit higher than the front rows, so passengers in the back seats get a better view.

Left: Intamin has produced *Superman: Ride of Steel* hypercoasters for Six Flags Darien Lake, Six Flags America, and Six Flags New England. Pictured here, as it dives into a misty maw, is the Six Flags New England model, considered by aficionados to be the choicest of the three because of its more dynamic layout and larger first drop (221 feet [67.4m] versus 205 feet [62.5m] for the other two).

Below: After *Magnum XL-200's* explosive premiere, Arrow Dynamics went on to build even larger hyper-coasters, including *Desperado*, a 225-foot- (68.6m) tall monster that runs a complete ring around Buffalo Bill's Hotel & Casino in Primm, Nevada. Riders actually board inside the casino.

But Sonny Boy's not done thrashing yet. There's spiral number two, a clockwise gyre, right in front of us. It's not quite as large or as intense as the first, but it's still plenty ferocious. Traveling at a headlong clip, we plow through this clockwise cacophony deep in the shadows of the gargantuan lift structure.

Then we give up the chase, dropping out of the second helix, rising over a gentle bluff, and whip-ping around 180 degrees. There's the finale, a tasty final drop, and then we leap back up to the load station's elevation.

It may not be as long as the *The Beast*, but this wild child can never be called Junior.

Giga-Coasters

Stealing the crown from the hypercoasters is a behemoth called the giga-coaster, a shocking, mind-warping marvel that is truly an extreme machine. Beyond everything we've looked at so far are roller coasters that affect our mind, body, and spirit in ways almost no other amusement park attraction can rival. Bigger, faster, steeper, they're not just coasters; they are nightmares made real. What precisely defines the nightmare that is a giga-coaster? That would be any roller coaster with a maximum height above 300 feet (91.5m). You read that correctly—that's 100 feet (30m) taller than hypercoasters.

Millennium Force

Cedar Point, the park that gave the world its first hypercoaster in 1989, broke records again in 2000 with the world's first giga-coaster. The Point's $25 million, Intamin-designed *Millennium Force* achieves its giga-coaster status with a lift hill that looms 310 feet (94.5m) above planet Earth. Adding insult to injury, *Millennium Force*'s first 300-foot (91.5m) drop gets as steep as 80 degrees. Top speed? An obscene 93 miles per hour (149.5kph).

In the barest sense, *Millennium Force* is a "standard" roller coaster; we're carried up a hill sitting in a two-per-row train, and once we're over the first peak, gravity takes it from there. But this coaster sports a fair amount of wonky technology, such as amazing lift mechanicals.

Necessity being the mother of invention, *Millennium Force* came complete with a new elevator-cable system because a traditional chain loop would simply have weighed too much (remember that *Magnum*'s lift chain tips the scales at 7 tons (6.3t), and it's only two-thirds as tall). So Intamin engineered what is essentially a big towline attached to a drum beneath the lift hill. The towline runs from the drum up to the summit of the hill and down its aggressively steep 45-degree slope into the station.

As a train engages the end of the towline, a computer system that regulates the apparatus powers up an 800-horsepower motor that drives a set of sprocketed gears connected to the drum. The gears shift, the drum turns, the cable is reeled in, and the train cars are dragged skyward very quickly.

Not only are the mechanisms towing the cars of interest, but so are the vehicles themselves. They are the same open-air trains that run on Intamin's

Above: Cedar Point's *Millennium Force* giga-coaster rockets out of its second tunnel, approaching a quick bunny hop alongside the station and one last overbanked turn before hitting the brake run.

Right: Looking up from below, it's easy to see how far *Millennium Force* tips its trains over around several turns. The steepest of them are over-banked a full 122 degrees off horizontal, meaning riders' heads are closer to the ground than their feet.

several *Superman: The Ride* hypercoasters (at Six Flags Darien Lake, Six Flags America, and Six Flags New England). The rear seats are slightly raised, allowing for a better view from those positions. With almost nothing in the way of sidewalls, it's all clear off to the left- and right-hand sides....

We follow two bits of advice: 1) wait for the front seat and 2) wait for the front seat. Why? For starters, we can savor how abruptly the cobalt blue box-beam track angles toward the sky right out of the station. We also get to watch as the towline slithers down underneath the low-slung nose of the lead car.

The coaster cars begin to move; all smooth and quiet, the cable drags us a foot or two (30.5 or 61cm). Without warning, we start jamming up that immense incline, tipping *way* back. We've got only about twenty-two seconds before we aren't going up anymore, so we look around. On the right is all of Cedar Point with its endless thrill-ride smorgasbord—mere Tinkertoys from the heights we reach in a heartbeat. On the left: water and more water. Eyes front, it's nothing but the top getting closer and closer, far faster than we probably want it to.

Climbing to 280, 290, 300 feet (85, 88.5, 91.5m)...we start to level off. As our car glides over the top of *Millennium Force*'s voluptuous 310-foot (94.5m) apex, the horizon rises. And rises.

And rises.

Soon we can't see the horizon anymore—because we're looking almost straight down.

We feel all of creation screaming up at us as we hurtle over this abominable precipice and experience several merciless, synapse-blasting seconds of near free fall. It isn't a completely vertical descent, but our mental protractors will measure it that way as we rage down what is likely the greatest first drop on any coaster, of any kind, ever built.

Rocketing like a bullet train, we plow through a long, sweeping valley only to soar up into the first of the *Force*'s signature overbanked turns, 122 degrees off horizontal, 169 feet (51.5m) above the soil. So smooth, so graceful, not a jolt, not a single shimmy, just wheel-smoking speed as we rise up and twist, lean over, and keep right on rolling like there was no tomorrow.

Diving back down, we skim over the planet's crust, shoot through a bend, and race into our first tunnel. Out of the darkness and into the light, we whip right up to the top of this coaster's second-greatest elevation, a 182-foot- (55.5m) tall lip-smacker (less than 20 feet [6m] shy of *Magnum*'s claim to fame) where, yes, airtime is in abundance. In the back it's just fine, but in the front it's simply divine. Nothing shocking or severe, just a sweet, gradual floater, like a negative-G palate cleanser before we move on to the *Force*'s twisterlike second course.

Over the coaster's isolated island, we lunge nearly to ground level again and enter an insane

Below: Cedar Point is jam-packed with record-breaking thrill rides. Although from this aerial view, the white *Power Tower* appears taller than *Millennium Force*, in reality it shoots riders up only 240 feet (73m) versus *Millennium Force*'s 310-foot (94.5m) peak.

Right: Although a giga-coaster, *Steel Dragon 2000* is primarily an out-and-backer, but between the "out" and the "back," there's a healthy serving of "twister" thrown in for good measure. From a height of 210 feet (64m), riders blaze down a swooping descent to hit 80 miles per hour (128.5kph) and rip around a tremendous banked helix.

pretzel-shaped whirlwind, hustling nonstop into another elevated, overbanked turn. It's poetry in motion.

Down, around, and back up again, through still another overbanked turn, careening this way and that, ascending and descending, still moving with furious intensity, yet never hitting a millimeter of track that doesn't feel just right. Every steel coaster, no matter how big or small, should run like this puppy.

Leaving the island behind, we vault over a smaller hill that gets our bodies airborne again, and we cruise down into a second tunnel, carving through a sharp turn to the left. Up alongside the boarding station, there's a bunny hop awaitin', and we do some rump-raising one last time.

A short straightaway sends the train whistling into a final whoop-de-do U-turn and we glide into the electromagnetic clutches of Intamin's high-tech brake run. Stunning is the only word for it.

Steel Dragon 2000

Millennium Force did not remain the world's tallest and fastest full-circuit coaster for very long. Only months after the *Force* unseated Magic Mountain's *Goliath* as the international drop and speed title-holder in May of 2000, Japan's Nagashima Spa Land honored the Asian calendar's Year of the Dragon with the $51 million, Morgan Manufacturing–designed *Steel Dragon 2000*, the world's second giga-coaster. Four records were broken on August 1, 2000, when this fire-belching fiend officially began its reign of terror: height, 318.26 feet (97m); first vertical drop, 306.77 feet (93.5m); length, 8,133 feet (2,479m); speed, 95 miles per hour (153kph).

Want some more bloodcurdling numbers? This 8,000-ton (7,256t) leviathan's second hill stands a mind-boggling 252 feet (77m) tall. And at the far end of *Steel Dragon 2000*'s awesome course,

D.H. Morgan Manufacturing, Inc.

Dana Morgan, cofounder of D.H. Morgan Manufacturing, is another designer with a sterling thrill-ride pedigree: his father is Ed Morgan, one of Arrow Development's founders. The younger Morgan has spent nearly his entire life in the amusement business, working at both Disneyland and Arrow, where he was part of the team that created the original *Corkscrew*. In 1983, after serving for seven years as general manager of the Santa Cruz Beach Boardwalk amusement park and a short stint as president of Arrow Huss (another precursor of today's Arrow Dynamics), he and his wife formed D.H. Morgan Manufacturing.

The nascent firm's first assignment was to build new trains for the classic *Giant Dipper* coaster at the Santa Cruz Beach Boardwalk, but today Morgan delivers far more than just coaster components. The company's current catalog includes boat rides; electric cars; monorails; people movers; a unique enclosed-vehicle, spinning flat ride called the 8-Ball; kiddie rides; mine-train coasters; and carousels (for the Islands of Adventure theme park at Universal Studios Escape in Orlando, Morgan produced the magnificent Caro-Seuss-El interactive merry-go-round).

Then there are Morgan's glorious hypercoasters. In the latter half of the 1990s, Morgan built a trio of these more than 200-foot- (61m) tall joyrides, and each of them can be found on most top ten coaster lists: *Wild Thing* at Minnesota's Valleyfair!, *Steel Force* at Pennsylvania's Dorney Park, and *Mamba* at Missouri's Worlds of Fun. Courtesy of Morgan coaster designer Steve Okamoto, Morgan hypercoasters are gloriously smooth and loaded with airtime.

This company's major 1999 endeavor was the *Steel Eel*, a 150-foot- (45.5m) tall creature at SeaWorld in San Antonio, Texas, and 2000 saw the firm build something far larger than it had ever tackled before: *Steel Dragon 2000*, once the world's tallest, longest, and fastest full-circuit coaster.

Today, Morgan is now part of Chance-Morgan Coasters, Inc., having joined forces in 2001 with Chance Industries, another well-known amusement ride manufacturer.

riders skyrocket all the way back up above 210 feet (64m) to enter this out-and-backer's madcap turn-around, a tornado of inclined spirals. Even at the halfway point, the *Dragon*'s streaking trains are still running with enough gusto to hit more than 80 miles per hour (128.5kph) at the bottom of the third descent.

As Morgan Manufacturing's senior ride engineer Steve Okamoto describes it, "After the first fifty seconds you will have traveled over 4,100 feet [1,250m], averaging over 55 miles per hour [88.5kph]. During that time you will have accelerated to speeds over 65 miles per hour [104.5kph] five times, while more than half of that time you will be traveling over 60 miles per hour [96.5kph] and you still have over thirty seconds of ride to go, with eight bumps and two tunnels. When you finish the 8,133-foot [2,479m] circuit, you will have dropped almost 1,200 feet [366m]." Yikes.

Free Fall

Extreme machines defy normal coaster classification in many ways. Sometimes they simply exceed previous limits of height, distance, or velocity. Other times, their extremes are measured by raw fear factor or the speed at which your stomach rises into your throat. This is the case with vertically dropping coasters. You don't always need a whole 360-degree inversion to generate intense reactions; a well-crafted 90-degree vertical drop is more than enough to make you squeal with delight.

Oblivion

A fine example of an extreme vertical drop can be found in Alton Towers' outlandish *Oblivion*, the first of Bolliger & Mabillard's Diving Machine roller

coasters, erected in 1998. Located in Alton, Staffordshire, the United Kingdom's Alton Towers is quite different from your typical American-style theme park. First, because of zoning regulations, no attraction in the park may rise above treetop level. So as you drive up to Alton Towers' entrance through the rolling English countryside, there's not a single telltale roller coaster peak, towering parachute drop, or spinning Ferris wheel to be seen. Second, once you've entered the well-manicured grounds, you immediately realize that the property did not begin life as a theme park; its central landmark is a beautiful manor house complete with lavish gardens.

Above: After emerging from *Oblivion's* subterranean tunnel, the coaster's sixteen-passenger shuttles careen around a turn and dip before rising to meet the brakes.

The hill beneath Alton Towers, once known as Bunbury or Bonebury, has been occupied by one group or another since as far back as 1000 B.C., when it hosted a small Iron Age community. But Alton's modern-day history really began at the turn of the nineteenth century, when the fifteenth Earl of Schrewsbury, Lord Charles, took an interest in upgrading the Alton estate, property that came with his title. Eventually, he and his wife moved onto the estate and Lord Charles began the extensive work of creating Alton Tower's famous Gardens, a huge project that consumed his attention for more than thirteen years until his death in 1827. Was Lord Charles much of a thrill seeker? We can't say for sure. But there's no way the Earl could have imagined what his beloved Gardens would someday become: home to an internationally recognized thrill-ride cornucopia.

The stringent building requirements and zoning regulations have forced Alton Towers to come up with some imaginative solutions when installing major rides—if you can't build up, then you've got to build down (you'll recall that *Nemesis*, the park's inverted coaster mentioned in chapter two, solved this problem splendidly). *Oblivion* makes a subterranean excursion of its own, so you won't be seeing any lift hills from a distance.

Follow the crowds right up to the imposing gateway of Alton Towers' X Sector, a raw steel and concrete thrill-ride zone that has all the cuddly warmth of a secret military base. It looks like the kind of place where technofetish supervillains are busy hatching plans for global domination (no surprise, given that John Wardley—a consultant director to the Tussauds Group, owners of Alton Towers, and the man responsible for *Oblivion*'s superb concept design—developed special effects for five James Bond movies).

As you step through that gate, you can see it only several yards away—*Oblivion*'s infamous vertical dive (it isn't purely 90 degrees, but it's awfully—and I mean *awfully*—close, almost 88 degrees).

Standing in the center of the X Sector courtyard, you can make a full 360-degree turn and survey the bulk of *Oblivion*'s 1,223-foot- (373m) long course. A steep chain lift hill rises up and out of the bunkerlike loading station. After making a small-radius turn to the left, the dark metal rails point south and disappear into the mouth of *Oblivion*'s "crater." Continuing underground, the track re-emerges out of a small pond and makes a highly banked turn. Finally, there's a small dip and a rise, the closing stunt that feeds *Oblivion*'s shuttles onto the brake run.

Speaking of the shuttles, these freakish coaster trains are among the oddest thrill-ride vehicles you'll ever board. Each of *Oblivion*'s black-and-orange cars features two rows of seats, eight across, bolted onto a rectangular metal platform. Of course, this seating pattern was designed to afford every passenger a clear view straight ahead (or, more precisely, straight down), and it makes for a truly unique conveyance (each shuttle, the single most expensive component of the ride, had a sticker price of £180,000 (about $257,438).

Before entering the queue, you can get a really close look at *Oblivion* committing its vile deeds, for just behind the X Sector's Rehydrator Café is an unadorned viewing area around the fenced-in crater. The area is perfectly designed to bring out the gawker in all. Tip your cranium skyward and watch as the shuttles get released, listening with evil glee at all the frenzied screaming. Ghastly.

The queue guides riders through the bunker with some amusing distractions along the way. At one point, the path enters a tunnel beneath a small hill, and there you will hear a prerecorded exchange between one very menacing Big Brother–ish voice and a much more frantic individual. It starts off something like this:

Big Brother: "Remain calm. There is nothing to fear."

Frantic Individual: "'Nothing to fear?' Then why is it called '*Oblivion*?!'"

The dialogue continues in this vein and sets a nicely paranoid tone for the whole affair....

Our march comes to an end inside the loading bay. Clambering across the wide aisles of the massive shuttle feels very unnatural; there's never been a sit-down roller coaster with leg room like this. Once we slide into our seats, however, there is a tiny bit of reassuring familiarity—these B&M cradles are standard issue and they are as comfy as ever.

Once the shoulder harnesses come down and the ride operators flash their thumbs-up for release, all sense of comfort evaporates. The shuttle rolls forward and then tilts back as it climbs to *Oblivion*'s summit. When the vehicle levels off to make the turn, it does not accelerate. Rather, it seems to slow to an agonizing crawl, making the inexorable approach to the drop even more terrifying. As we inch forward, engaging a second chain drive, the one that will hold us motionless above our impending doom, we can't help but admire Mr. Wardley for his brilliant sense of drama. This is psychological torture, pure and simple, and it makes our hearts pound like jackhammers.

At long last, the shuttle begins to tip over. Peering down into the narrow maw of *Oblivion*'s crater is to stare into the black core of fear itself. We begin to scream, our bodies bracing for the fall, when the shuttle freezes in place. For one long, horrible four-second interval, everything is still. Then a disembodied voice echoes around us: "Don't...look...*down*."

Opposite: If the idea of riding Alton Towers' vertical-drop *Oblivion* is more than you can bear, entertain yourself by getting a look as the coaster's shuttles plummet into a subterranean tunnel.

Right: Straight up one side and straight down the other, the Thrust Air 2000 does things no other roller coaster before it has ever attempted. The first production model of this phenomenal ride opened in 2000 at Paramount's Kings Dominion as the *HyperSonic XLC* (Xtreme Launch Coaster).

We drop.

Words cannot convey the absolute brutality of it all: nose-diving almost 197 feet (60m), much of it straight down, hitting 68 miles per hour (109.5kph), the air ripping at us as the shuttle falls like a dead weight—that, my friends, is one *hell* of a rush. Underground, the track curves back up, fighting our downward progress with almost 5 Gs worth of force. We burst back into daylight, soar into the turn, drop, climb, and glide to a halt. All too brief, but it's completely bonkers.

Oblivion was a tremendous undertaking, both technically and financially. It required nine engineers, twelve draftsmen, ninety-two welders, sixty-eight fitters, fifty-seven machinists, twenty-three painters, and twenty quality-control experts to shape 42 tons (38t) of steel into this first-of-its-kind machine. All told, there are forty sections of track, twenty columns, and 5,550 bolts. The final bill for the effort came to approximately £12,000,000 (about $16,829,187). To date, Bolliger & Mabillard has been hired to supply only two other Diving Machines: *G5* at Janfusun Fancyworld in Taiwan and *SheiKra* at Busch Gardens Tampa in Florida. While *G5* is close in layout to *Oblivion, SheiKra,* which opened in 2005, is a whole other beast entirely. You'll hear more about *that* coaster in the last chapter.

Blast Off!

We can thank Utah's S&S Power (the two initials stand for Stan and Sandy Checketts, the husband and wife team behind S&S) for expanding the thrills of free-fall tower rides to a coaster with a perfect 90-degree drop. Prior to S&S' technological embellishments, free-fall rides had typically begun with vehicles making a leisurely climb to their final drop positions; S&S' Space Shot tower, first made public in 1995, turned that notion completely on its head.

This new contrivance harnessed explosive blasts of compressed air to literally shoot octagonal passenger carts straight up a freestanding square steel tower with startling force.

At the base of each Space Shot, an Ingersoll-Rand screw-type compressor pumps dried, refrigerated air into a 2,000-gallon (7,570L) storage tank located within the tower structure. The passenger rigs are connected by cables to pistons at the top of four vertical cylinders that rise to the peak of each tower. Blastoff occurs when computer-controlled gate valves open and the pressurized air floods into those cylinders, ramming the pistons

S&S Power, Inc.

Stan Checketts, president and founder of S&S Power, Inc., the company responsible for the Thrust Air 2000 coaster, was a furniture- and cabinetmaker for several decades. But he had long harbored a yearning to craft something with a little more oomph than dining room tables. He has confessed, "I have had the same dream for thirty years...to somehow throw people high in the air by using towers." Checketts was inspired by a game played with his offspring: "It might sound wild, but the concept actually evolved from tossing my nine children in the air when they were little kids. I used to think, 'there has to be a way to do this on a grander scale.'" Looking back, "grander scale" becomes a whopping understatement.

The first steps were taken in 1989, when Stan and his wife, Sandy, founded Sports Tower, Inc., erecting vertical bungee-jump pillars. These attractions were hugely popular, but they were just the beginning. In January 1993, their second enterprise, S&S Sports, Inc., began fabricating the Trampoline Thing, a bungee-cord/trampoline combo that sprouted by the hundreds around the globe. Not long after, Checketts and his staff began developing the attraction that would place them firmly in the annals of stomach-knotting horror: in early 1994, their third corporation, S&S Power, Inc., was formed, and from that venture the Space Shot free-fall ride was born.

Some hundred-plus Space Shots, Turbo Drops, and Double Shots later (Double Shots being smaller "thrust-up" and "thrust-down" free-fall towers), S&S finally got into the coaster business with the Thrust Air 2000. Man, does it "throw people high in the air" something fierce.

S&S promises that it has even more new thrill-ride concepts in the works, including something that they've said is more terrifying than anything they've ever created. Be afraid—be *very* afraid.

downward with cables firmly in tow. The upshot, so to speak, is this: riders are yanked skyward with a force of nearly 5 Gs, instantaneously accelerating to as much as 50 miles per hour (80.5kph). The launch from the base of a Space Shot is so sudden, so ferocious, that just watching it happen makes your hair stand on end. The free fall back down starts with a little kick, too; while the decelerating carts are still rising, the cables interrupt the climb and begin to pull them back down, providing an instant of *less* than zero gravity and lifting riders right out of their seats. This, my friends, is quite simply airtime heaven.

In 1997, an even more wig-flipping version was introduced: the Turbo Drop. Using the same technology as a Space Shot, a Turbo Drop carries you up at an unbearably slow pace, allowing you to savor the knee-weakening heights to which you're climbing. Once at the top, you're held motionless for several long seconds, knuckles bone white. This time, the savage blast fires you straight down at faster than free-fall acceleration. From 0 to 40 miles per hour (64kph) in the blink of an eye, you're sent flying out of your seat and firmly against the shoulder harnesses; it's the kind of moment for incontinence undergarments.

Right: The solitary 165-foot- (50.0m) tall hill of the Thrust Air 2000 prototype punctures the skies over S&S Power's Logan, Utah, factory and proving grounds. With its 1.8 second, 0 to 80-mile-per-hour (128.7kph) launch, the compressed-air-powered cars literally pushed roller coasters to new extremes.

With that gruesome record of achievement behind it, in 1999 S&S unveiled the Thrust Air 2000 prototype to introduce several roller coaster design innovations. First and foremost, as its name implies, Thrust Air 2000 takes advantage of the Space Shot's compressed-air system to shove its vehicles into action. Second, its trains ride atop large-diameter pneumatic tires and shock absorbers. Last, the track itself is fabricated with specially designed I-beam rails. According to S&S, all of this adds up to a coaster that is smoother, quieter, more cost-effective, more energy-efficient, more maintenance-friendly, and, yes, more intense than any other coaster on the market. How

intense? Try 0 to 80 miles per hour (128.5kph) in 1.8 seconds.

On the morning of October 19, 1999, the Thrust Air 2000 made its debut. Just as the sun was making its way into the sky, a group of journalists and several members of the American Coaster Enthusiasts were shuttled out to the S&S plant. Before we'd gotten to within several blocks of the facility, Thrust Air 2000's single hill became visible; dazzling white against the clear blue sky, it was about 165 feet (50m) tall, straight up one side and straight down the other. It was like the kind of hyper-exaggerated version of a roller coaster you'd see in a Saturday morning cartoon—but this was real.

Thrust Air 2000's Ingersoll-Rand compressors fired up, and an empty vehicle crept its way around the first turn toward the launch strip, where it came to a stop. A single warning buzzer rang, followed by a hollow *whoooosh*, the sound of wind coursing through cylinders. Then, in the blink of an eye, the train screamed forward.

All eyes followed as it surged through the first vertical curve and made that hysterical 90-degree climb. Snaking over the apex, it plummeted back down. Lord have mercy because now it's time for a manned flight.

After boarding on a raised wooden deck at one end of the prototype's oval course, the train inched forward over a row of friction wheels. Once around a left-hand bend, the vehicle came to a halt alongside the exterior wall of the factory. Up ahead, a drag strip "Christmas tree" of lights hung to the right of the rails. Beyond that was the vertical tower.

The recorded growl of a revving car motor signaled that we were about to bust a move. The warning alarm blared and the Christmas tree lit up, a row of beacons counting down to green—toes curled, knuckles whitened, skin crawled, heart stopped.

Whooooosh. "Here we go!"

Before my mind could register that we'd begun moving, we were already halfway to the base of the tower and gaining speed at an appalling rate. I'll probably never get to ride in a fighter jet as it's getting hurled off the deck of an aircraft carrier, but it doesn't matter; this is close enough. As I hollered my bicuspids loose, we blasted into the curve and, smooth as can be, made the first 90-degree change of direction. Pulling away from Mother Earth, the train made an effortless climb to that 170-foot (52m) peak like it was headed all the way to Jupiter.

We lost just enough speed to make a gentle trip over the top. With such a small radius, this upended U-turn was a freaky treat; one moment, we were looking at nothing but sky, and the next, we were facing right back down.

And down we dove, with all the fury of an unimpeded free fall. Magnificent.

It took almost one and a half years for the Thrust Air 2000 to move from prototype to production model, but in spring 2001, Paramount's Kings Dominion proudly debuted the *HyperSonic XLC*, the world's first ready-for-prime-time Thrust Air 2000. It is similar in most respects to the prototype, but there were some modifications. First, the radius of

Above: The compressed-air-launched rocket sled forces another set of riders to experience Thrust Air 2000's face-first, vertical descent. Paramount's Kings Dominion's *HyperSonic XLC*, the first Thrust Air 2000 to open to the public, features a 90-degree plunge that's not quite as severe, but the production vehicles are equipped solely with lap restraints, not over-the-shoulder harnesses.

the descent curve was made larger, so the 90-degree fall is not quite as long. On the plus side, the test vehicle's over-the-shoulder harnesses were replaced with lap restraints, and the rest of the layout, formerly just a simple oval, now includes a few additional curves and a bunny hop.

But the *HyperSonic XLC* is only a kiddie coaster compared to what S&S Power has planned for the Thrust Air 2000. Know this: S&S can build versions more than twice as high—that's around 350 feet (106.5m)—and will be able to push vehicles to speeds far faster than 100 miles per hour (161kph). Hardly child's play.

Reverse Free Fall

In December 1994, as thrill-ride speed and height records were being shattered with increasing regularity, amusement parks around the globe were ever more eager to develop the first 100-mph (161kph) attraction, an engineering feat and public relations coup without equal. To get coaster cars moving at that hellacious speed, Intamin had come up with the idea to use linear synchronous motors (LSMs), which are somewhat similar to but more complex than the LIM systems employed on *Volcano* and *Batman & Robin: The Chiller*. Further, what Intamin proposed to create was a gargantuan L-shaped structure. A long horizontal straightaway, lined with LSMs, would accelerate passenger vehicles from 0 to 100 miles per hour (161kph) in about seven seconds, providing them with enough momentum to climb nearly 400 feet (122m) straight up. At that point, gravity would take over and riders would free-fall *backward*, experiencing an atrocious six and a half seconds of weightlessness. The rather dry term Intamin applied to this widget was a Reverse Free Fall (a turn of phrase that strikes me as similar to the way scientists once referred to atomic bombs as "physics packages").

Superman: The Escape

Any park attraction, Thrust Air coaster or not, that does attain velocities beyond 100 miles per hour (161kph) will only be following in the footsteps of what is, for now, the tallest and fastest thrill ride in the world. That extreme machine is Six Flags Magic Mountain's *Superman: The Escape*, a twin-tracked, 415-foot- (126.5m) tall, 100-mph (161kph) monstrosity.

Six Flags was more than up to the challenge to build a Reverse Free Fall, and Magic Mountain, already home to some of the greatest thrill rides in the world, was deemed the place to put this proto-type through its paces. Time Warner, then owner of the Six Flags theme parks, had begun actively developing a new *Superman* feature film and recognized the synergy in creating this kind of ride with a related theme. Checks were signed and the nuts-and-bolts work began.

The park announced with great fanfare that *Superman: The Escape* would open in May 1996. To worldwide dismay, it did not. Weeks of delay turned into months, and thrill seekers were left panting in anticipation.

The causes for the delay were all related to the LSM launch system. LIM systems are essentially passive; their electromagnetic fields operate like spinning tires, pushing the train along from one motor to the next. An LSM system is more efficient, yet requires a vastly more complex interaction between the motors and the ride vehicle. *Superman*'s custom 6-ton (5.4t), fifteen-passenger cars carry not simple metal fins but huge magnets. As the magnets pass each motor, the motors

Opposite: *Superman: The Escape*'s riders are thrust from 0 to 100 miles per hour (161kph) in about seven seconds, climbing a 415-foot (126.5m) vertical tower. And then they must free-fall nearly 400 feet (121.9m) *backwards.*

Left: Known by Intamin, its creators, as a "Reverse Free Fall," Six Flags Magic Mountain's *Superman: The Escape* (pictured) is one of only two 100-mile-per-hour (161kph) thrill rides on the planet. A second Reverse Free-fall exists at Australia's Dreamworld theme park, a single-track model dubbed *Tower of Terror.*

Right: The world's tallest and fastest thrill ride of any kind built to date, Six Flags Magic Mountain's awe-inspiring *Superman: The Escape* looms 415 feet (126.5m) over this roller coaster–packed park.

adjust their energy cycles to coordinate with the energy cycles of the magnets, like the intermeshing of two spinning gears. Of course, this interaction happens within microseconds, and getting the timing right is no simple matter. Each LSM in the chain has to be turned on and off at an absolutely precise moment. Test after test was needed to get the timing down, and special software had to be written and revised again and again to control the power delivery to such a fine degree.

Then the issue was electricity—a whole mess of it. To get each 6-ton (5.4t) car hustling along, those motors need serious juice: 1.2 megawatts per track. The park had to run a dedicated line off Southern California Edison's local grid just to feed this beast.

Getting extra power into the park was one thing; getting it into the motors was even trickier. Engineers encountered a problem called the skin effect—the wattage was so great that electricity traveled along only the outer surface of the wires, denying the motors the supply they needed. So the initial set of wires had to be replaced with larger diameter cables.

If you think this all sounds pretty intense, you're in good company: NASA, the folks that shoot stuff up into space, actively followed *Superman: The Escape*'s development with an eye toward applying a similar system to their space-shuttle launch procedure. Could cut down on fuel costs, they say.

Slowly but surely, Six Flags Magic Mountain's engineers began to bring the attraction up to speed: 70, 80, 90 miles per hour (112.5, 128.5, 145kph). In January 1997, a 100-mph (161kph) launch was achieved. Had I been present, I'd have cried tears of joy. Finally, on March 15, 1997, *Superman* officially took flight.

Today, the job of operating *Superman: The Escape* is a simple affair. Once the thumbs-up is

given for launch, the main operator and remote operator simultaneously press buttons on their consoles (sort of like launching a nuclear warhead), and those 6-ton (5.4t) cars take off with a skull-shattering 2,000 horsepower at their disposal.

There was some debate among the thrill-seeking community about just how to classify this pleasure device. Call it a roller coaster, call it a free-fall tower, call it an instrument of torture—it doesn't really matter to me. What does matter is that *Superman: The Escape* offers an experience once available only to our finest jet pilots. After my first trip, all I could whimper was "I gotta do that again!" It totally, utterly, *completely* rules.

When you approach Six Flags Magic Mountain from the south on Interstate 5, the first thing you spot beyond the hills surrounding the park is the observation deck of the 38-story Sky Tower. Before 1996, that's all you would have seen. Now, further up, poking higher into the heavens, is the vertical steel structure of *Superman: The Escape*.

I don't care how much you may have heard about its size; once you actually see what 415 feet (126.5m) really means, it takes your breath away.

When you enter the park, stop and listen: "Gee, I didn't think there were any naval bases nearby. Where are those F-16s coming from?" You can't imagine the noise this thing makes. Stand under the bend in the far end of the track and wait for a car to pass overhead—it is *earsplitting*.

Follow the trails up to Samurai Summit, and there you'll find a miniature version of *Superman*'s Fortress of Solitude. The line snakes inside the icy

Below: Togo's largest U.S. coaster is the massive, looping *Manhattan Express* at the New York–New York Hotel and Casino in Las Vegas, Nevada. Its taxicab-themed trains run over a course that completely encircles the main structure of the resort. And though its largest drop is just 144 feet (43.9m), its lift hill goes all the way to 203 feet (61.9m), earning it hyper-coaster status.

Right: Before *Superman: The Escape* opened at Six Flags Magic Mountain, *Revolution*, also designed by Intamin, was the park's main attraction. Known more grandly as the *Great American Revolution* when the ride opened in 1976, it was the first modern vertical looping coaster. This brilliant ride (along with Arrow's Corkscrew coaster) was like a match to gasoline, igniting a firestorm of creativity that has resulted in the hundreds of looping steel roller coasters we're blessed with today.

cavern, where it forks in two. Makes no difference which way you head, really—you'll get a fine view from either track. The dimly lit corridor leads into an anteroom just outside the Launch Chamber. Inside this room, you can hear, but not witness, the departure: there's an unearthly whine, a split second of screaming, and then silence. Whatever happens in there is happening horrifically fast. It's not unheard of for tentative riders to reach this point and decide to bail, even after a two-hour wait.

A row of automated doors opens and admits a carload at a time. The trick, I think, is to finagle an aisle seat; that allows for an unobstructed look at the horizon when the car reaches its maximum altitude. Once your hindquarters are planted, you may find yourself pawing around for a seat belt or shoulder harness. Guess what? There isn't one—just a simple lap bar. Yes, it is perfectly acceptable to freak out at this point. One woman I rode with that first time needed some reassuring from the nearest ride operator before we were allowed to leave. Once settled, wave bye-bye, and don't blink or you'll miss it....

There's nothing left to do but lean your noggin against the headrest and say your prayers. The car drifts forward, almost floating, so you have one heartbeat to try and brace yourself—and then it happens.

One second, you're stationary; the next, you're ripping along that 900-foot (274m) track like your life depended on it. Your adrenal glands go berserk, and if this doesn't make you scream like a rabid monkey, you're probably unconscious. Faster and faster, it's a long, smooth rush. The force pushing against your back is simply awesome—4.5 Gs worth. Seven seconds after this chaos has begun, you're traveling at that magic 100 miles per hour (161kph) and ready to get vertical.

The car surges through the curve, and your nose points 90 degrees off horizontal: Up, up, and away! Higher, higher, higher…it's almost literally out of this world. Gradually, gravity wins. You stop, and now's when you want to look to your side and see what this very Magic Mountain looks like from roughly 400 feet (122m) aboveground. Holy Toledo, that is something to tell the grandkids about. Remember, you're up twice as high as Niagara Falls. Then it's time to head back down—six and a half seconds, utterly weightless, *backward*. Wrench your hands from the bar to hold a penny in your open palms and watch what happens.

By the time you hit the curve, you're doing the triple-digit bop again, but the miracle of eddy current braking—a frictionless electromagnetic process that slows the cars down—starts to cool things off, and you cruise back into the Fortress of Solitude. Perhaps only twenty seconds have passed, but your life will never be the same again.

Tower of Terror

While *Superman* underwent its final stages of tinkering, Intamin erected a slightly smaller, single-track version of its Reverse Free Fall at Australia's Dreamworld: the ghoulishly postapocalyptic *Tower of Terror*. After walking through the gaping mouth of a 36-foot- (11m) high, crimson-eyed metallic skull, riders must tread over uneven steel floors through the collapsing remains of some huge industrial facility. Twisted steel girders strain to hold up the cracked rock and concrete walls; steam gushes from broken metal pipes; dim lights behind the crumbling ruins cast jagged shadows—the scene is terribly horrific.

A decrepit cargo elevator takes passengers up to the final boarding area, and they're left with only one way out: hopping into a spiked and studded heavy-metal hot rod, like something out of the movie *Death Race 2000.*

On February 7, 1997, Dreamworld announced that during an independent test, verified by a local justice of the peace, a police-calibrated, handheld Falcon radar gun officially measured the *Tower of Terror* at 100 miles per hour (161kph), making it the first thrill ride in the world to successfully carry passengers to that phenomenal velocity. Yes, it beat *Superman* to the punch, but Magic Mountain's double-whammy Reverse Free Fall remains the taller of the two. And for reasons that will soon become clear, it may be the last Reverse Free Fall ever built.

Impulse Coasters

As forward and backward shuttle coasters go, *Superman: The Escape* is certainly without peer, sizewise. But Intamin has created another type of shuttler that, diminutive as it might be in comparison to *Superman*, is nearly as well equipped in the

dread-delivery department. Intamin calls it an Impulse coaster.

This particular device is distantly related to Paramount's Kings Dominion's *Volcano: The Blast Coaster*; like *Volcano*, impulse coasters are inverted, LIM-powered machines, with two-across vehicles—but the comparisons end there. The first of these off-the-wall wonders to open in the United States was dubbed *Superman Ultimate Escape*, taking up residence at Ohio's Six Flags Worlds of Adventure. It's there today still, but both park and coaster have new names (sort of). The attraction is now called *Steel Venom* and the park has returned to its original moniker, Geauga Lake, since its sale in 2004 to Cedar Fair. Identity issues aside, you'll find *Steel Venom* standing right up against Geauga Lake's roadside border, so it's the first coaster you see while driving up to the parking lot—and it's a traffic stopper like few others.

There isn't much to eyeball, really—just two sections of red vertical steel rails bookending a long

horizontal straightaway. The rear spire is all neat and even. But that front spire—an amoebic tendril coiling up, up, and far away from the bulky blue pipe sections that support its lower half, this wacky track brings one adjective to mind: fragile.

Several tons of coaster train and cargo climbing and torquing around that flimsy spiral, nearly 180 feet (55m) off the ground? It takes a lot to really spook me these days, but the sight of this thing had me spooked from here till Tuesday. It's so easy to imagine the dreadful sounds of metal creaking, rending, and shattering like porcelain.

As with nearly all forward-backward shuttle coasters, there are benefits to riding in both the very front and very rear seats. You may need to swallow hard, but go with the front first....

Hopping into the molded blue booty-scoop and pulling down the yellow shoulder harness, we face that long straightaway—track and station canopy above, cement platform below. Sitting squarely beneath the first contorted minaret, there's a slope-roofed metal enclosure—and that's all we can see.

Waiting for the launch, we're wondering how close to the top of that spire we're going to get. "Hey, did you notice any brakes up there?" The load crew moves out of harm's way.

Thumbs up, boogie down.

WHAM! We hurtle forward madly, raging toward the first vertical curve. Over the park's go-cart course we fly, and up we soar. The nose of the lead car gains enough altitude to get into a little twist 'n' shout, but we don't ascend to anywhere near the pinnacle before gravity slows us and starts pulling us back. Someone says, "Well, now, that wasn't so bad."

Oh, just wait.

Screaming backward through the station, we get another LIM boost and rocket up the rear tower. Sweet view from the front, looking right back down at the ground. There's a split-second pause before we're falling face-forward.

The train blasts back through the loading dock, and we can feel those pernicious LIMs really pour it on, giving us an even meaner push. The moment we return to the base of the forward arm, now traveling at *Steel Venom*'s sizzling 70-mph (112.5kph) maximum velocity, we're well aware that we're about to go higher than we did our first trip—a whole lot higher.

Up through the curve, we motor skyward and begin whipping around to the left. The folks in the stern may not be all that concerned, but we, leading the charge, can see how rapidly we're approaching the end of the line—and we're still pinwheeling and climbing. "Stop, stop, stop, *stop* already!" To those watching from the ground as the train seems to be on its way to a catastrophic malfunction, it looks bad. From the front seat of that rampaging train, it is unconditionally horrifying.

We do finally halt. Plummeting away from what looks like certain derailment is a most wonderful sensation. But the terror isn't over yet.

Back through the station we scramble, and up the rear tower we roll, higher and higher, and soon, we hit that zero-G float, ready to drop. We don't. THUNK! A powerful set of brakes holds us there.

Falling forward into the harness, we hang for a brutal instant, poised 90 degrees off horizontal and staring straight down.

It's that second rear climb that makes the back row nearly as perverse a pleasure as the front. When we get fully elevated and those brakes bite down like a pit bull and hold us at their mercy, we're so much higher up than we were in the forward car. We take a look to the side while we're

Togo

Togo is Japan's foremost thrill-ride supplier, having sold more than nine hundred different attractions to parks around the world since getting started in 1935 (the company's first roller coaster, constructed in 1953, is Japan's oldest operating coaster). With a diverse product line that includes Ferris wheels, Skycycles, monorails, dark rides, water rides, kiddie rides, and more, Togo is a one-stop shop for all our thrill-ride needs. But Togo's international reputation is primarily due to its several steel coaster innovations.

In 1984, Togo created *King Cobra*, America's first stand-up coaster, for Paramount's Kings Island. Just two years later, they followed that break-the-mold attraction with the righteously peculiar *Ultra-Twister*, built for Six Flags Great Adventure in Jackson, New Jersey. Now located at Six Flags Astroworld in Houston, the ultrarare *Ultra-Twister* drops riders down a nearly vertical plunge and then spins them through several heartline spirals, both forward and backward.

In 1995, Togo took the heartline inversion concept further with its first continuous-circuit heartline coaster: *Viper*, again delivered to Six Flags Great Adventure. A far more impressive heartline coaster, the *Manhattan Express*, was the scream machine centerpiece for the New York, New York Hotel and Casino in Las Vegas when it opened in 1997. That 203-foot- (62m) tall hypercoaster features a wild twist-and-dive inversion, one that can't be found anywhere else in the United States. Last but not least, Togo's 259-foot- (79m) tall *Fujiyama*, a monstrous twister that looms over Fujikyu Highland in Japan, reigned as the world's tallest and fastest full-circuit coaster for several years.

praying that those shoulder restraints don't fail... and thinking about where we're going to find a clean pair of pants.

Oh, and here's one last detail to tickle our innards: when the brakes on the rear tower release the train after the second climb, the tower *sways*.

This Impulse coaster's ability to make our blood run cold wasn't lost on Six Flags. For 2001, two more of these rabble-rousers were ordered and sent to Illinois' Six Flags Great America and California's Six Flags Marine World, where they do us in as *V2: Vertical Velocity*. I'm sure that won't be the last of them, either.

Stratosphere

Though many will scoff at the inclusion of this last attraction in the extreme-machines class, I can't help but mention it here: the *Let It Ride High Roller*. Indeed, it's downright puny; you can find dozens of children's coasters with larger drops, faster speeds, and more intensity. So what makes the *Let It Ride High Roller* extreme? It's perched more than 900 feet (274m) off the ground.

This act of mad genius was the work of Bob Stupak, developer of Las Vegas' Stratosphere, a $550 million hotel and casino megaresort that's home to America's tallest freestanding observation tower. It was Stupak's inspiration that led to the installation of the world's highest thrill rides, the zany *Let It Ride High Roller* coaster and the *Big Shot*, a free-fall tower. At first Stupak was told that it couldn't be done, but the visionaries at Structures and Machines Constructions, an Italian engineering firm, said they could deliver the *High Roller*, and the aforementioned S&S Power team came through with the *Big Shot*.

The Stratosphere's casino and hotel are at the base of the tower. The tower's elevated twelve-story "pod" contains indoor and outdoor observation decks, a cocktail lounge, a revolving restaurant, conference and meeting rooms, and, of course, wedding chapels.

But the real action is on Level 12A. There, 921 feet (28.5m) up, is where we board the *Let It Ride High Roller*. All it does is circle around and around the outside of the tower's crown—gentle dips, a little lift hill, and that's about it. If you took it down to sea level, you'd have yourself the dullest coaster ever conceived.

But it's not at sea level. For anyone who suffers from even the mildest case of acrophobia (I'm afraid I'm in that category, believe it or not), the *Let It Ride High Roller* is as petrifying as coasters come. The seats are equipped with over-the-shoulder harnesses, so you're strapped in as safe and sound as possible. But riding in the outer row, the one that puts you closest to the edge—well, that's something I'll always let my riding companion do.

If you disembark the *High Roller* yawning and want to get your heart racing, there's always the *Big Shot*, probably the scariest thrill ride known to mankind, which shoots you 160 feet (49m) up to a final altitude of about 1,081 feet (329.5m). I've never hollered louder or harder, and I did it without an ounce of shame.

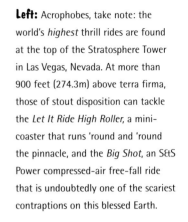
Left: Acrophobes, take note: the world's *highest* thrill rides are found at the top of the Stratosphere Tower in Las Vegas, Nevada. At more than 900 feet (274.3m) above terra firma, those of stout disposition can tackle the *Let It Ride High Roller*, a mini-coaster that runs 'round and 'round the pinnacle, and the *Big Shot*, an S&S Power compressed-air free-fall ride that is undoubtedly one of the scariest contraptions on this blessed Earth.

ROCKET COASTERS

CHAPTER 5

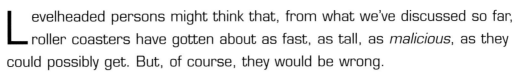

Levelheaded persons might think that, from what we've discussed so far, roller coasters have gotten about as fast, as tall, as *malicious*, as they could possibly get. But, of course, they would be wrong.

On June 6, 2002, California's Knott's Berry Farm became the lucky park to usher in a new subspecies of launched coaster—the Rocket Coaster—gussied up as *Xcelerator*, a 1950s hot-rod-themed screamer. Through the magic of Intamin's new hydraulic launch system, unique to the Rocket Coaster, *Xcelerator* hustles its trains from zero to 82 miles per hour in 2.3 seconds down a 157-foot-long straightaway. At maximum velocity, those trains then begin a cloud-bound excursion with a 90-degree twist to the right and continue scrambling all the way to 205 feet, where they peel over what is now commonly referred to as a "top hat" element. (Top hats are vertical U-turns and can be negotiated either on the inside—as does the Batman half of Six Flags Great Adventure's *The Chiller*, resulting in the train going upside down—or on the outside, as does *Xcelerator*.) With a second 90-degree twist on the descent side of the top hat, *Xcelerator* freefalls back down and shreds through some elevated turns before hitting the brakes.

While vertical hills are wild aplenty, it is *Xcelerator's* white-hot acceleration that catches the jaded thrill seeker off guard. And here's how the Rocket Coaster does its very naughty business: reservoirs feed low-pressure hydraulic fluid into a collection of pumps, which then pressurizes the fluid and sends it off to piston accumulators. When the Rocket Coaster's launch begins, the piston accumulators' valves open and release the pressurized fluid into motors (as many as *48* of them) that drive an enormous winch at the end of the horizontal launch track. Wrapped around the winch are cables attached to a "catch car" that rides on its own set of rails beneath the launch track. A small hook, or "dog," drops down from each train into a pocket in the catch car, so that when the winch starts spinning, it reels in the catch car, which in turn pushes the train forward...really, really, *really* quickly. (So quickly, in fact, that it would seem the days of Intamin's linear synchronous motor-launched Reverse Free Falls are truly over.)

Xcelerator is indeed an Xtreme machine. But just one year later, Cedar Point trumped that attraction—and all others...*again*—with a Rocket Coaster so off-the-charts immense, it created yet another height category: the Strata-Coaster, as in "nearly hits the stratosphere."

Left: Knott's Berry Farm's *Xcelerator*, shown here as it races around a wide turn, was the first of Intamin's new Rocket Coasters, and though it isn't even half as tall as those that have followed, it's still a major rush, with a zero to 82 mile per hour launch in less than three seconds. And its flame-adorned, early-muscle-car-themed trains, to use the language of the era, really "razz my berries, man" (meaning, they impress me).

Top Thrill Dragster

After the Point broke through the 300-foot ceiling with *Millennium Force*, I was certain that many, many years would pass before the next major height barrier—400 feet—would be surpassed, if ever. But in 2003, Cedar Point did just that with *Top Thrill Dragster*, a Rocket Coaster with a top hat 420 feet tall. Feeling woozy? It gets worse. *Top Thrill Dragster* also hits 120 miles per hour—in *four seconds*.

Cedar Point's skyline is now completely dominated by *Dragster's* soaring yellow and red superstructure. Even *Millennium Force* seems, well, kinda small now. (If you really want to give yourself the willies, hang around till after dark and look at this coaster when it's all lit up, glowing against the night sky.) Oh, and how's this for worrisome? At more than one location in the queue, we're informed that, "Occasionally, a launched train will not clear the hill. You should not be concerned; the train will slowly return to the launch position." Gulp.

Should you need a place to sit and reconsider your decision to ride, there's the set of metal bleachers that faces the launch zone. You'll be mightily entertained by watching how each passenger squirms, yelps, freezes and/or freaks just before takeoff. From this vantage point, you'll also get to appreciate how much effort was made in designing this coaster's unique trains. The "stadium seat"-equipped middle cars are not much different from those found on *Millennium Force*. But the first and last cars, each with just a single two-passenger row, are unique to *TTD*. The sleek winged nose in front and the faux racing engine and air foil in back make these cargo-haulers as distinctive as they come.

Non-riders will also dig the delightful details of the launch. Each train moves slowly into position accompanied by the prerecorded rumbles of an idling high-horsepower engine. Occasionally, the engine "revs" a bit—*vroom, vroom*—a sweet little tease. Finally, the long row of metal fins that line the launch track—an integral part of *TTD's* fail-safe magnetic braking system—sinks. The train inches forward.

Buh-bye.

To the tune of a roaring engine and squealing tires, and a very nifty cloud of "burning rubber" smoke, the train *disappears*. Unnerving to watch, but nothing like what it is to ride.

You won't truly grasp just how tall *TTD's* tower is until you are sitting in a train, waiting to roll out of the station, knowing that in a very short time, you will be up on top of that monster. Out into bright sunlight we roll, coming to a stop alongside the bleachers. *Vroom, vroom.*

Waiting, waiting. *Vroom.*

The train rolls about two inches forward. Deep in our souls, we know that the next dozen or so seconds of our lives are going to be brutal.

Vroom!

O n e ... We start to move. Very fast. Those who aren't yet screaming begin doing so.

T w o ... We must be traveling at 80 miles per hour and the train just keeps on accelerating like it's got solid-propellant rockets on board. Every alarm in the nervous system is wailing at Red Alert volume.

T h r e e ... screaming becomes impossible. Unqualified terror and the forces pummeling our bodies literally strangle us into silence. We're still accelerating.

F o u r ... Knifing through the air, the train hits 120 brain-splattering miles per hour. And now things really go berserk.

F i v e ... We rip up the first vertical curve to about 150 feet in altitude, and climb ever higher, straight into the firmament, with stupefying speed.

S i x ... The track spins us to the right and we

regain the ability to scream. Higher, higher, higher.

S e v e n ... We're just about at the summit. Keep your eyes open, lest you miss a view you'll remember till your dying days, no matter how hard you try to forget.

E i g h t ... Four hundred and twenty feet above all creation, the nose of our vehicle swings up and over the top, dragging us right along behind it. Sweet mother of mercy... There's *Millennium Force*. Way down below us. And now it's time to drop, at 90 degrees, from over 400 feet. Abandon all hope.

N i n e ... We dive towards the planet, once again hurtling to nearly twice the legal speed limit.

T e n ... The train pinwheels through a 270-degree track twist, narrowly slicing past big, yellow supports in an ever-increasing blur. Whipping around and falling hard, it feels like we're going to drill our way clear through to the earth's core.

E l e v e n ... At flesh-rippling velocity, we start to pull out of the dive.

T w e l v e ... Back to a far saner distance from solid ground, the train levels off and begins to decelerate, smooth as glass: 110 mph, 90, 70, 50, 30...

And finally, we crawl to a stop. About 15 seconds and it's over, fifteen seconds of abominable intensity unmatched by any other roller coaster anywhere. If Hell has thrill rides, this brilliantly evil machine should be one of them.

But, believe it or not, there's already something *even bigger*.

Storm Runner

The next Rocket Coaster to come along was, mercifully, not quite as unruly. In 2004, Pennsylvania's Hersheypark inducted its speediest roller coaster to date, *Storm Runner*. And while it's not nearly as

Opposite: Coming out of a 270-degree track twist, riders on Cedar Point's *Top Thrill Dragster* are clearly feeling exultant, having just survived a 120 mile per hour launch and a climb to 42 stories above the ground. Does it look like there's a lot of screaming going on? Yes, it sure does, doesn't it?

fast, nor as quick, nor as tall as its cousins, this pocket Rocket does something its predecessors don't: it goes upside-down.

Those familiar with Rockets really start paying attention once seated in a train. These puppies have shoulder harnesses, not what we're used to. But they are as comfortable as can be expected and quite necessary, as will soon be discovered. Sitting up close to the front, you'll likely be thinking, "man, that launch track is short." Yes, *Storm Runner* gets right down to business without wasting a moment. We roll forward to the go-zone and stop. The metal deceleration fins that line the rails drop...the train drifts backwards...and then the storm breaks.

The push at our backs is strong, not lung-collapsing (like *Dragster's*), but it's a laugh riot nonetheless. In two seconds, we're at 72 miles per hour and before we know it, we're looking up at the heavens—and entering them—mighty quick.

Like usual, this Rocket spins us 90 degrees as we climb, this time to the right. And, like usual, we scurry over the top—staring at the sky, staring at the horizon, staring straight down—lickety-split. But from here on in, there's no more "like usual."

The train shrieks down 180 feet, straight and true all the way, hitting *Storm Runner's* top speed of 75 miles per hour. And with all that momentum to spare, we surge right back up. And up. And *over*, 135 feet above the terrain. Pulling out of the inversion, we flip and plummet to the side in a very nice bit of aerobatics. Call it an Immelman, call it a Cobra Loop, call it whatever you'd like. Whatever it is, it's *all right*. And it's just a warm-up for what's coming next.

Peeling out of the bottom of the Immelman/ Cobra Loop, we head back up and level off to whip through a one-two punch of corkscrewy pleasure.

Stengel Engineering

If there is one person who has influenced the world of modern roller coasters more than any other, it is Germany's Werner Stengel, an engineer whose career has spanned four decades. During that time, Mr. Stengel and his cohorts have been involved with the development of more than *460* roller coasters, from kiddie machines up to Six Flags Great Adventure's record-crushing *Kingda Ka* (along with flume rides, dark rides, Ferris wheels, bumper cars, monorails, and just about every other type of ride you can imagine). As design and engineering consultants, they've worked with almost every major ride manufacturer, and the only continent that doesn't host a single Stengel-assisted attraction is Antarctica.

The sheer quantity of their output is remarkable, but the quality of Stengel Engineering's work is equally impressive. Quite a few of the remarkable roller coasters discussed in this book would not be what they are without Stengel's contributions, including *Riddler's Revenge* and *Goliath* (Six Flags Magic Mountain), *Oblivion* (Alton Towers), *Millennium Force* and *Top Thrill Dragster* (Cedar Point), *Volcano: The Blast Coaster* (Paramount's Kings Dominion), and many more.

Mr. Stengel retired from daily practice in 2001 but still works closely with his firm. As a measure of his enduring impact, in 2003 he was bestowed with the International Association of Amusement Parks and Attractions' "Hall of Fame Living Legend Award." And in October 2005, Stengel received an honorary doctorate from Sweden's Göteborg University, "for his inexhaustible creativity in linking physics and design to the experience of the body in roller coasters and other rides." No wonder many call him the "Roller Coaster Guru."

Opposite: Hersheypark's *Storm Runner*, the first Rocket coaster to include inversions, flogs riders with three loopy contortions, the last of which is shown here: its one-of-a-kind "flying snake dive." Riders in the rear of the train will most appreciate this highly disorienting element.

We start with inversion two, a super-elevated heartline roll, far, far above the throngs below. Our vehicle tips over to the starboard side, gently tossing us into those shoulder harnesses.

There's some choice hangtime way up there, rolling over and over until we're back upright for a second. But it is only a second before we enter the last inversion, an element that has been crowned a "flying snake dive," and it is *Storm Runner's* signature moment.

We continue to spin around the horizontal axis but by the time we get completely inverted again, we've already begun to descend and rip to the left. It's somewhat like the Cobra Loop we've just encountered, but far more intense. The inversion seems longer-lasting and the drop far steeper, making it one heck of a mind-twisting way to fall from the sky.

And once we regain some sort of normal posture, *Storm Runner* pulls us through a grand sweep of a valley, scoots up, and pitches us to the right before sliding down the final brake run. Short, perhaps, but very, very sweet.

Kingda Ka

How long did *Top Thrill Dragster* remain the tallest and fastest thrill ride on the planet? Just two years. Yes, for 2005, Six Flags Great Adventure commissioned a Rocket Coaster that would dethrone *TTD* as the king. It's 456 feet tall. It accelerates from zero to 128 miles per hour in 3.5 seconds. And it's called *Kingda Ka.*

Kingda Ka is the anchor attraction for a whole new 11-acre themed area christened "The Golden Kingdom," a mythical jungle realm with "Balin's Jungleland," a play area with rides for the pint-sized set, and "Temple of the Tiger," an edu-tainment exhibit with a 33,000-square-foot Bengal tiger arena and an amphitheater that presents the "Spirit of the Tiger" show dedicated to exotic creatures such as albino pythons, macaws, capuchin monkeys, and—of course—Bengal tigers. It's all about as striking an environment as a Six Flags park has ever created, 456-foot-tall roller coaster notwithstanding.

Beyond out-muscling *Top Thrill Dragster* in stature and speed, the blue and green *Kingda Ka* has a couple of distinctive upgrades. First, the boarding station is twin-tracked, with parallel load platforms (a feature shared with *Storm Runner*). Second, instead of a horizontal brake run, this Strata-Coaster cools things off with a gently-sloped 129-foot-tall camelback hill. But for all intents and purposes, *Kingda Ka* is a near-twin for *TTD* and that means you're in for the same "*Mommy, make it stop!*" acceleration, and a view from the top that is beyond belief.

You'll have an idea of what you're in for the moment you pull into Great Adventure's parking lot, for on your left is the entire profile of *Kingda Ka* in all its grisly majesty. Should you choose to ride, you'll soon be looking back down at that parking lot

from a vantage point normally reserved for migrating birds. As a frame of reference, consider that Great Adventure's second-largest roller coaster, *Nitro*, is half as tall.

But to really understand what 456 feet means, I recommend the following exercise. If you live in a major metropolitan area, you'll probably have ready access to a building over 45 stories in height. Go to the 45th floor, find a window, and press your face up against the glass. And just stare out for a minute, thinking about what might happen should the glass break...

The Rocket Coaster has become as much in vogue around the world as it has in the U.S. In 2005, Sweden's Liseberg fired off *Kanonen* (Swedish for "cannon"), a 46-mile-per-hour junior model with a 78-foot-tall top hat hill and a vertical loop; England's Alton Towers released *Rita—Queen of Speed*, a 61-mile-per-hour model with no truly major hills, but a twisting, turning course 2,099 feet long; and Madrid's Warner Bros. Movie World unleashed *Superman: Escape*, a themed Rocket with a 62-mile-per-hour launch and a 131-foot-tall top hat.

More are on their way. Norway's TusenFryd has announced *Speed Monster* for 2006, a 55.9-mile-per-hour model that will feature an Immelman inversion and a corkscrew. And England's second Rocket is also already under construction at Thorpe Park, though as of this writing, its name is still a mystery. But it will be a mini-version of *Kingda Ka*, with a 205-foot top hat (and successive camelback) after a 2.5-second, 80-mile-per-hour launch.

Left: This is it, folks, the largest roller coaster "hill" presently known to man. Six Flags Great Adventure's *Kingda Ka* adds another 36 feet to *Top Thrill Dragster*'s humbling 420-foot physique to max out at a record-trashing 456 feet. Never has a coaster train looked so very, very small. And yet, lines to board are among the longest in the park, indicating that we've still not hit the limit of what thrill seekers will tolerate. One can only imagine if and when a roller coaster will depose *Kingda Ka* as the king of all coasters.

AFTERSHOCK

CHAPTER 6

The chronicle of the roller coaster has a definite beginning, but the end of the coaster's evolution is nowhere in sight. In the months and years to come, we will continue to see new scream machines that will inch us closer to the limits of human endurance and further stretch the boundaries of what can be defined as a roller coaster.

Consider just the last few years. In late December 2001, Japan's Fujikyu Highlands debuted *Dodonpa*, the second of S&S Power's extraordinary Thrust Air coasters. While its major hill is about 170 feet tall, only a few feet higher than Paramount's Kings Dominion's *HyperSonic XLC* (the first Thrust Air), *Dodonpa* improved upon its predecessor by ramming its trains from zero to nearly 107 miles per hour (172kph) in less than two seconds. Then in 2003, Cedar Point's *Top Thrill Dragster* came along, hitting 120 miles per hour and hot-rodding up to 420 feet. And in 2005, Six Flags Great Adventure's *Kingda Ka* roared all the way to 128 miles per hour and 456 feet into the firmament. That's quite a pace of achievement.

Speed and height records haven't been the only statistics to change. In March 2002, England's Thorpe Park unveiled *Colossus*, the planet's first ten-inversion coaster. Designed by Intamin, this nearly 100-foot-tall loop decathlon packs one vertical loop, one double-inversion cobra roll, two corkscrews, four counter-clockwise heartline spins, and one clockwise heartline spin into its 2,788-foot (850m) -long course. Remember, that's *two* more inversions than previous loop-packed coasters have ever dared to deliver.

But there's much, much more. What follows are some of the latest and greatest attractions as of spring 2006.

Flying Coasters

While Vekoma's Flying Dutchman first introduced us to this particular mode of thrill seeking, Bolliger & Mabillard is enjoying great success with its own Flying coaster. Debuting in 2002 was Alton Towers' *AIR*, another thrill ride designed in conjunction with John Wardley, B&M's co-conspirator for Alton Towers' provocative *Oblivion*. While not a record-breaker by any means, this two-inversion, 65-foot-tall, 2,756-foot-long skydiver is notable for introducing B&M's unique and typically innovative interpretation of the flying coaster; B&M's flyers differ from Vekoma's Flying Dutchmen by loading their passengers standing upright, with trains hanging below the track. Once the restraints are secure, the rear of each car swings up, pulling riders into the prone and face-down flight position right in the station.

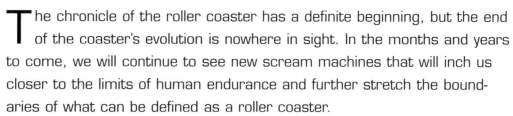

Left: Only two years after Vekoma engineered the world's first "flying" coaster, Bolliger & Mabillard slip-streamed right behind them with a pair of their own flyers in 2002— *AIR* at England's Alton Towers and Six Flags Over Georgia's *Superman: Ultimate Flight* (pictured here). Two more Supermen took to the skies in 2003 at Six Flags Great Adventure in New Jersey and Six Flags Great America in Illinois. And in 2006, a unique Bolliger & Mabillard flyer is poised to wing its way over Six Flags Magic Mountain in California.

Right: Dorney Park's *Wild Mouse*, in Allentown, Pennsylvania, is a picture-perfect example of the time-honored Wild Mouse archetype: four-passenger cars whizzing across a "top shelf" of switchback turns and then scampering over a series of punchy drops down below. The Screaming Squirrel adds a new twist by turning this layout on its side.

Just one month later, in April 2002, the U.S. got its own B&M flyer, dubbed *Superman: Ultimate Flight*, at Six Flags Over Georgia. At 115 feet in height, *SUF* is far taller than *AIR* and sports the world's first Pretzel Loop inversion, a dizzying piece of aerial acrobatics that looks in profile much like the crunchy, salted snack from which it borrows its name. In essence, it's a vertical loop turned upside down; we enter and exit the massive upright oval from the top, not the bottom, a feat never achieved before.

Since then, both Six Flags Great Adventure in New Jersey and Six Flags Great America in Illinois have sent bodies (and spirits) soaring with their own *Superman* clones and more are guaranteed to follow.

Screaming Squirrel

Stan "The Man" Checketts and his S&S Power posse have, yet again, created a roller coaster that makes one simply say, "No *way*." The Screaming Squirrel, as goofy as it sounds, is related most closely to Wild Mouse coasters, those mini-machines that feature an elevated deck with row after row of straightaways and hairpin, 180-degree turns. But instead of zigzagging back and forth on a horizontal plane, the way we do riding Mice, the Squirrel has us zigzagging back and forth *vertically*.

After climbing a 65-degree lift hill to maximum altitude, each four-passenger car creeps over the top and rolls down a slight ramp towards the opposite end, where we dive over the edge and keep on flipping around until we're completely upside down and rolling back in the opposite direction, like a squirrel scampering along the underside of a tree branch (I'm sure we'll never be more thankful for shoulder harnesses). And then we drop and flip upright. And then get flipped upside down again, and on and on until we reach the bottom.

The first of these wacky contraptions went into real-world operation in 2005 at Italy's Gardaland

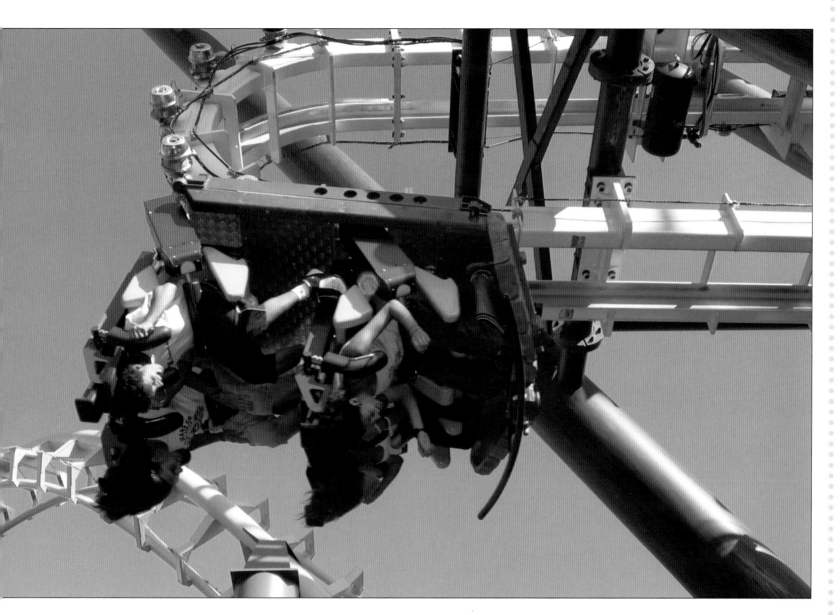

Left: S&S Power's first active-duty Screaming Squirrel coaster, *Sequoia Adventure*, tosses its riders into their shoulder restraints at Italy's Gardaland park, where they'll spend the next few seconds completely upside-down. This dizzy madness happens three times before they get to the bottom. As of this writing, *Sequoia Adventure* is the only such coaster of its type in operation, but should the concept prove popular, we'll see many more; the Screaming Squirrel's small footprint makes it ideal for just about any amusement park.

park as the 98-plus-foot-tall *Sequoia Adventure*. Dressed up in a forest-lumberjack theme, *Sequoia Adventure* delivers three full flip-flopping twists, keeping riders upside down for nearly *half of the descent*...that sounds pretty adventurous to me.

Woodies

While steel coasters are still blooming with far more frequency than time-honored woodies, parks in America and beyond have harvested some remarkable lumber-railed wig shredders in the last

couple of years. In 2004, Tennessee's Dollywood theme park installed its first woodie, and they went for the gusto with *Thunderhead*, a barnstormer of Byzantine complexity from Great Coasters International. This super-twister—100 feet tall and 3,230 feet long—manages to send its two Millennium Flyer trains thundering at a top speed of 54 miles per hour through a sumptuous course of warped drops and steep curves, criss-crossing through its own structure *32* times, and delivering a first for a coaster of any kind: a "fly-through" of *Thunderhead's* loading dock where the trains make

Below and Opposite: The Gravity Group, a new wooden coaster developer, made one mighty splash with its first installation: the hair-raising *Hades*, at Mt. Olympus Theme Park in Wisconsin. Long, fast, and loaded with underground surprises (including hidden banked turns that pretty much lay the train on its side), *Hades* announced to the world that the Gravity Group is ready and willing to earn our love and respect. And they most certainly will with this coaster and *The Voyage*, Holiday World's 2006 addition, a woodie that will gobble up 6,442 feet of track, making it the third-longest wooden coaster on the planet.

a 40-mile-per-hour dash just eight feet over the exit ramp. It's not uncommon to hear this coaster referred to as "the best woodie in America" with firm conviction.

Prior to designing *Thunderhead*, GCI was called upon to work their magic for Branson, Missouri's new Celebration City theme park (a sister park to Dollywood and Branson's own Silver Dollar City) and they responded with the *Ozark Wildcat*, which opened with Celebration City in 2003. While smaller by every measure than *Thunderhead*, this sharp-clawed kitty has still earned many fans with its 540-degree spiral of a first drop and plenty of track-twisting anarchy.

S&S Power's new wooden coaster division has had a promising start with *J2* (short for *Jack Rabbit 2*) at Clementon Amusement Park in New Jersey, *Avalanche* at Timber Falls Adventure Park in Wisconsin, *Timberhawk: Ride of Prey* at Wild Waves and Enchanted Village in Washington, and *Falken* at Fårup Sommerland in Denmark. *J2*, the largest of the quartet, stands 110 feet tall, and

boasts a first drop of 105 feet at 62 degrees, making it one of the steeper woodies you'll find.

Intamin is a name not often associated with woodies, but they do engineer them, and their latest is a major twister: *Balder* at Sweden's Liseberg park. Named for the Scandinavian god of justice (and the son of Frigg and Odin, Scandinavian gods themselves), this impressive 118-foot-tall, 3,511-foot-long woodie was the largest single investment in the park's 80-year history when it opened in 2003.

In 2005, the Gravity Group made its presence known with *Hades*, a steel-structured woodie at Mt. Olympus Theme Park in Wisconsin. (If "Mt. Olympus Theme Park" sounds unfamiliar, that's because until 2003 the place was known as Big Chief's Carts and Coasters.) A true heavyweight contender, *Hades* starts off with a 140-foot drop down a record 65-degree slope right into a subterranean chasm. The rest of its 4,726-foot-long course, packed with the steepest banked curves of any wooden coaster (some just about *vertical*), includes more than enough underground travel to earn its hellish title.

And while *Hades* is pretty impressive, the Gravity Group's next coaster should be even more so. Opening on May 6, 2006, at Holiday World and Splashin' Safari is *The Voyage*, a 6,442-foot-long marvel that will anchor the park's new Thanksgiving zone. Along with measuring up as the third longest woodie anywhere, *The Voyage* is loaded with superlatives: its first 154-foot plunge will be among the steepest for a wooden coaster at 66 degrees; it will include eight underground descents through five tunnels, a record; its many hills will deliver a whopping 24.2 seconds of combined airtime, another record; there will be two 90-degree banked turns; and its top speed will be 67.4 miles per hour.

But the biggest news for 2006, woodie-wise, is Six Flags Great Adventure's *El Toro*, the first Intamin-developed wooden coaster to hit the United States. And hit it will, as the second tallest and fastest wooden coaster on the Continental 48. Coming up just shy of Kings Island's *Son of Beast*, *El Toro* will stand 181 feet tall and send its trains down a 176-foot drop, angled at a sizzling 76 degrees, by far the steepest decline on a wooden coaster, *ever* (a mere 14 degrees off completely vertical). Stampeding at a top speed of 70 miles per hour, this out-and-back and twister combo should be a fine compliment to the park's only other woodie, the twin-tracked *Rolling Thunder*, which it will stand right alongside in a newly developed themed area called "Plaza del Carnaval." To think this park is adding such a tremendous attraction just one year after the premier of *Kingda Ka*... most excellent.

Impulse Coasters

Just about every card-carrying thrill seeker will be pleased to hear that Intamin's nasty Impulse coasters, those inverted, LIM-powered shuttle hooligans, have found new homes. Following the pair of *V2: Vertical Velocity* attractions that opened in 2001 at Six Flags Great America and Six Flags Marine World in California (the latter having been redesigned the following year so that its forward, twisting spike is now angled instead of completely vertical), Cedar Point got a ferocious custom model in 2002 called *Wicked Twister*. This Impulse bucks tradition with twisted vertical track spirals at *both* ends of its course. Better still, those spirals are more twisted than ever before, with 450 degrees of total rotation (versus 360 degrees for the "stock" versions). And the *coup de grace*? They top off at 215 feet, making *Wicked Twister* the only hyper-Impulse running. Wicked, for sure.

Perhaps not quite as exciting, but good news nonetheless, Minnesota's Valleyfair! got its own standard Impulse in 2003, under the name *Steel Venom*.

X

Six Flags Magic Mountain's one-of-a-kind monster, the world's first "4th Dimension" coaster, is an Arrow Dynamics–designed thriller best described as the deviant offspring of a roller coaster and a somersaulting carnival ride. Its 5-ton (4.5t), 20-foot (6m) -wide vehicles (seven per train) feature two pairs of leg-dangling seats extending like wings off either side of the track structure. Each seat—brace yourself—is capable of full 360-degree rotations, both forward and backward, controlled by the 4th Dimension's groundbreaking rail system. But wait—there's more: *X* is a hypercoaster. Riders plummet over its near-vertical, 215-foot drop *head down and face first*, reaching a top speed of 76 miles per hour (122km/h). The rest of the 3,610-foot (1,100m) -long course has us spinning, whirling,

scrambling, and screaming over front flips, back flips, and two enormous vertical curves called "raven turns."

Though it opened to the public in early 2002, *X* was plagued with operational problems, no surprise given this prototype's audacious engineering. But after a couple of months of downtime and some tweaking, it reopened in August 2002 to deservedly rapturous acclaim.

Now that Arrow is a part of S&S Power, it's certain that the 4th Dimension concept will evolve and, hopefully, more models will arrive sooner than later. There's a very good chance that a second-generation 4th Dimension is targeted for a park in Japan. And that's not all; we may see something similar from our friends at Intamin, who are working on a rotating-vehicle coaster of their own.

Giant Inverted Boomerangs

Vekoma continues to push its shuttle coasters to ever greater extremes, and three of their next-generation inverted shuttlers, things they call Giant Inverted Boomerangs, have pierced the skies above the United States at Six Flags Magic Mountain, Six Flags Great America, and Six Flags Over Georgia. All three, under the moniker of *Déjà Vu*, are far more radical than their predecessors. Unlike the inverted train models Vekoma has produced to date, like Paramount's Kings Island's *Face/Off* and Six Flags

America's *Two-Face: The Flip Side*, this version's twin lift towers don't just angle up into the sky—they're completely vertical. And they're 196 feet (59.5m) tall. After being pulled into the heavens, riders drop down the first tower, reaching a top speed of 65 miles per hour (104.5km/h); whip through a 102-foot (31m) -tall vertical loop; and tackle a 110-foot (33.5m) -tall cobra roll. Then it's *Déjà Vu* all over again, *backward*: two 90-degree drops and six head-over-heels somersaults in one freaky package.

Since this trio of terror opened in 2001, Vekoma has sent a GIB to Europe. In 2002, the big

Boomer made its first appearance overseas as the *Stunt Fall*, at Warner Bros. Movie World in Spain.

Motorbike Launch Coasters

Had you ever wondered what it would be like to race a motorcycle over roller coaster rails? The folks at Vekoma did and they came up with another award-winning product, the Motorbike Launch Coaster. Riders straddle and are secured with a lower-back clamshell restraint onto a fairly authentic recreation of a horsepower-packed motorcycle to get hydraulically launched into action, from zero to top speed in about three seconds. The concept was first presented to potential buyers in 2003 and took the "Best New Product" Award at the October 2004 IAAPA trade show and the "Best Idea Euro Amusement Show 2004" that November. But by the time those awards had been bestowed, the first MLC was already revving its engines; in August 2004, *Booster Bike* opened at Toverland, in The Netherlands, with a train of eight side-by-side motorcycles, for a total of sixteen riders per train. Suitable for thrill seekers young and old, *Booster Bike* hits a top speed of 46.6 miles per hour and sprints over three camelback hills and several twists and turns before hitting the brakes.

Just about a year later, in August 2005, England's Flamingoland got an even peppier MLC (with a top speed of 54 miles per hour) christened *Velocity*. And it shouldn't be ages before we hear of even more Motorbike installations.

SheiKra

It was a long time coming, but the United States finally got its first Bolliger & Mabillard Diving Machine in May 2005 and, boy howdy, was it worth the wait. Busch Gardens Tampa's *SheiKra*,

which takes its name from an African hawk that plunges straight down at its quarry, differs from its antecedents (Alton Towers' *Oblivion* and Junfusun Fancyworld's *G5*) in several striking ways. Instead of a train with two rows of eight passengers, *SheiKra's* massive vehicles are *three* rows deep. And after its initial 200-foot vertical nose-dive (good enough to generate a maximum velocity of 70 miles per hour), this raptor attacks a 145-foot-tall Immelman inversion, the first time a coaster of this ilk has traveled completely upside-down. The fun's not over yet—peeling out of the Immelman, *SheiKra* makes a *second* 90-degree descent, this time about 138 feet down, right into a tunnel. And the finale is a straight-away through a shallow pond, with *SheiKra* hurling two cascading columns of water from its port and starboard stern, a visual treat for those gazing in wonder on the sidelines.

Along with being a scream machine of the highest order, *SheiKra* further illustrates Busch Gardens Tampa's inclination to bless its major coasters (which also include *Gwazi, Kumba* and *Montu*) with names you simply won't find anywhere else.

Themed Coasters

It's been a good time for roller coasters doing double-duty as high-speed dark rides, like Disneyland's *Space Mountain*. Originally opened in 1977, two years after its larger, twin-tracked cousin launched at Walt Disney World's Magic Kingdom in Florida, the single-course California version closed in 2003 for a floor-to-ceiling renovation with all-new steel rails and supports, new vehicles, new special effects, new *everything*, to reopen in summer 2005, just in time for Disneyland's 50th anniversary. And this groundbreaking trip through "the final frontier" is as space-tacular as ever.

In 2004, the two Universal Studios parks, in Hollywood, CA, and Orlando, FL, opened their first roller coasters, the *Revenge of the Mummy* attractions. Based upon "The Mummy" and its sequel "The Mummy Returns," these enclosed Premier-engineered whippersnappers start with a slow crawl through forbidden chambers. Once our presence is discovered, evil reanimated corpses go on the rampage and we're launched into a wild ride through the blackness. With both forward and backward motion, the thrills of linear induction motor thrusts, and

some pretty groovy ghoulies, these two multimillion-dollar spookfests are first-rate, scary fun.

For 2005, Paramount's Kings Island and Canada's Wonderland parks served up identical launched coasters (from Premier Rides) based on *The Italian Job* heist movie called *The Italian Job: Stunt Track*. With vehicles designed to look like the MINI Cooper automobiles that were featured in the film's notorious chase sequence, these coasters position us as stunt drivers careening through a perilous "screen test." Racing through a parking garage, diving down a stairwell, sprinting away from a menacing helicopter, crashing through a billboard, and splashing down in an aqueduct are just some of the highlights of these 40-mile-per-hour joyrides.

But opening in 2006 may be the most ambitious themed coaster ever created: *Expedition Everest*, at Walt Disney World's Animal Kingdom. With a budget in the neighborhood of $100 million, this wild train ride through the Himalayan peaks will take us, Everest trekkers, through all

come to an abrupt end, apparently leaving us nowhere to go. But then that platform tilts forward…and tilts…and tilts…until we're held completely vertical and the front of the rails engage with the rest of the course. And then we dive.

In 2002, Vekoma installed its first "Cliffhanger" tilt coaster at Discovery World, a park in Taichung, Taiwan, where it does psychic damage as *Gravity Max*. At 1,863 feet long, with just one vertical loop, *Gravity Max* may not sound like much. But imagine what it must be like to sit in the very front row as the train starts tipping forward about 100 feet off the ground…criminy.

Cantilevered Roller Coasters

For the fertile mind, there are always roads not yet traveled, and John Hogg, a longtime veteran of the theme park industry, has a *fertile* mind. Over many years, he has developed and refined a now-patented vision for the thrill ride of tomorrow, the Cantilevered Roller Coaster. Inspired by a Warner Bros. Roadrunner cartoon, wherein the tenacious Wile E. Coyote attempts to capture his nemesis on an Acme Rocket Sled, Hogg tried to imagine how he could put *us* on that runaway sled, in a detailed environment, out of control, even going airborne off the edge of a cliff. To make such an experience possible, Hogg set out to do two things: one, make the track nearly invisible to riders and, two, allow the vehicle to change elevation and skew laterally, independent from the principal direction of travel. And so was born the cantilevered notion.

A cantilever is a long bar or beam that is supported at one end and bears weight at the other. Hence, the cantilevered roller coaster vehicle sits at the top of the beam and the primary wheel chassis supports the bottom. There are two sets of rails, one atop the

manner of hazards including, but hardly limited to, unexpected plunges, a mad dash in reverse, and a face-to-furry-face encounter with a roaring yeti. With coaster mechanicals supplied by Vekoma, *Expedition Everest* will be the grandest attraction at any of the Walt Disney parks in Florida, its artificial mountain standing about 200 feet tall above the Animal Kingdom's Asia section. And with an 80-foot drop and a top speed of about 50 miles per hour, this roller coaster will be one of the most bona fide thrillers in Disney's arsenal. Lastly, we're promised that the yeti itself is going be one serious customer, with motion actuators that generate forces on the scale of a Boeing 747 jet engine. Egad.

Tilting-Platform Coasters

A completely out-of-control concept that's waiting to catch fire is the tilting-platform roller coaster. Pure and simple, at the highest point, the train comes to a stop on a horizontal platform. The track rails

The Gravity Group

After Custom Coasters, Inc. unexpectedly shut its doors in 2002, four of its former employees—Larry Bill, Chad Miller, Korey Kiepert, and Michael Graham— took off and started this new firm. The first couple of years, their operation focused on consulting for some existing coasters; in 2003, they designed and engineered a new transfer track for *The Raven* at Holiday World in Santa Claus, Indiana, allowing for two-train operation. That same year, they were also enlisted as roller coaster anima- tion consultants for *The Polar Express*, the big-budget computer animation spectacular starring Tom Hanks.

But they really came to the party in 2005, with their first all-new from the ground up woodie: *Hades* at Mt. Olympus Water & Theme Park in Wisconsin Dells, Wisconsin. With plenty of subterranean tunnels, the well-named *Hades* was as fine a debut as any company could want. And in May 2006, the company's sophomore effort, *The Voyage*, is scheduled to open at Holiday World, an event eagerly anticipated by coaster fans worldwide.

Anyone familiar with the Custom Coasters portfolio knows we should continue to expect big things from the Gravity Group.

other, and the bottom set of rails carries the primary wheel chassis. The upper rails act as a guide for a secondary wheel chassis through which the cantilever passes. And this secondary wheel chassis becomes a fulcrum, or point of support at which the cantilever can pivot. So by varying the vertical distance between the upper and lower rails, and by shifting the upper set of rails to the left or right of the lower set, all sorts of wild effects are possible.

For example, imagine the Roadrunner's desert recreated as a dark ride set. The entire rail system for the "Rocket Sled" would be placed below the set, and—save for the groove in the floor necessary for the cantilever to pass through—there would be no indication of where we'd be going (and with some creative lighting, that groove could be made very hard to see). At the start, the two rails would be as far apart vertically as possible, which would place the vehicle very close to the ground. But as the action kicked in, the bottom rails would rise, pushing the vehicle up, up, and away, as if it were taking flight over the desert floor.

Even without extensive theming, the concept would still provide some very unexpected thrills. With the upper railway partially concealing the lower, we'd never be quite sure of just what to expect. Suddenly we'd pitch to the left or right, or soar up off what appeared to be the rails controlling our journey.

Right now, the Cantilevered Roller Coaster is still on the digital drawing boards, but that may soon change. The next step requires a partnership between Team CRC (which also includes Hogg's wife, Barbara Kolo, and an ad hoc group of engineers, designers and assorted professionals) and a coaster manufacturer to develop a full-scale prototype. S&S Power, a company known for thinking *way* outside the box, has made overtures about forming just such a partnership. There has even

been a tentative approach from a "large park operator," although right now, the parks themselves are taking a "wait and see" attitude.

But should the CRC system prove viable, stand back and watch the floodgates open.

A Final Thought

So where do we go from here? Will roller coasters get even taller and faster than *Kingda Ka?* In the August 30, 2004 issue of *The New Yorker* magazine, in an article by Kevin Conley entitled, "How High Can You Go?" Daniel Keller, the general manager of Cedar Point, was quoted: "...there may be a manufacturer that will come up tomorrow and say 'We got a great concept on an eight-hundred-foot roller coaster.' We'd certainly want to take a look at it." Granted, given the expense to manufacture and construct such an outrage, we shouldn't be holding our breath for anything quite so massive.

And yet...

When the 310-foot-tall *Millennium Force* opened in 2000, I was fairly confident that we'd get nowhere near a roller coaster over 400 feet tall for quite some time—a decade, at least. But it happened within three years. And just two years beyond that, we're already closing in on 500 feet.

It would appear that the sky, as they say, is the limit.

Opposite: If you need to know how frightening Six Flags New Jersey's *Kingda Ka* Rocket Coaster truly is, then take a close look at this picture, a shot of the train on its way to the ozone layer. Note that every single rider has a firm grip on the harnesses. That's a rare sight indeed.

Appendix

Need to know where to go? What follows is a list of some of the biggest and best amusement parks in the United States and around the world, and just a sampling of the major coasters you'll find at each fun zone, including attractions discussed in this book, as of summer 2005.

The United States

Alabama

Visionland, Bessemer
Rampage
Zoomerang

Arizona

Castles 'n' Coasters, Phoenix
Desert Storm
Patriot

Arkansas

Magic Springs, Hot Springs
Arkansas Twister
Big Bad John
Gauntlet
New Coaster for 2006

California

Belmont Park, San Diego
Giant Dipper

Bonfante Gardens, Gilroy
Quicksilver Express

Disneyland, Anaheim
Big Thunder Mountain Railroad
Matterhorn
Space Mountain

Disney's California Adventure, Anaheim
California Screamin'
Mulholland Madness

Knott's Berry Farm, Buena Park
Boomerang
GhostRider
Montezooma's Revenge
Silver Bullet
Xcelerator

Paramount's Great America,
Santa Clara
Demon
Grizzly
Invertigo
Psycho Mouse
Top Gun
Vortex

Santa Cruz Beach Boardwalk
Giant Dipper

Six Flags Magic Mountain, Valencia
Batman—The Ride
Colossus
Déjà Vu
Gold Rusher
Goliath

Ninja
Psyclone
Revolution
Riddler's Revenge
Scream!
Superman: The Escape
Viper
X

Six Flags Marine World, Vallejo
Boomerang
Kong
Medusa
Roar
V2: Vertical Velocity
Zonga

SeaWorld San Diego
Journey to Atlantis

Universal Studios Hollywood
Revenge of the Mummy

Colorado

Lakeside Amusement Park, Denver
Cyclone

Six Flags Elitch Gardens, Denver
Boomerang
Flying Coaster
Half Pipe
Mind Eraser
Sidewinder
Twister II

Connecticut

Lake Compounce, Bristol
Boulderdash
Wildcat
Zoomerang

Florida

Busch Gardens Tampa
Gwazi
Kumba
Montu
Python
Scorpion
SheiKra

Cypress Gardens Adventure Park
Galaxy Spin
Starliner (name may change, opening 2006)
Triple Hurricane

SeaWorld Orlando
Journey To Atlantis
Kraken

Universal Studios Florida, Orlando
Revenge of the Mummy
Islands Of Adventure
The Incredible Hulk
Dueling Dragons

Walt Disney World Resort, Orlando
Magic Kingdom
Big Thunder Mountain Railroad
Space Mountain
Animal Kingdom
Expedition Everest (opening 2006)
Primeval Whirl
Disney-MGM Studios
Rock 'n' Roller Coaster

Georgia

Lake Winnepesaukah, Rossville
Cannonball

Six Flags Over Georgia, Atlanta
Batman—The Ride
Déjà Vu
Dahlogena Mine Train
Georgia Cyclone
Georgia Scorcher
Great American Scream Machine
Mind Bender
Ninja
Superman: Ultimate Flight

Wild Adventures, Valdosta
Boomerang
Cheetah
Hangman

Idaho

Silverwood Theme Park, Athol
Corkscrew
Timber Terror
Tremors

Illinois

Six Flags Great America, Gurnee
American Eagle
Batman—The Ride
Déjà Vu
Demon
Iron Wolf
Raging Bull
Superman: Ultimate Flight
V2: Vertical Velocity
Viper
Whizzer

Indiana

Holiday World, Santa Claus
Legend
Raven
The Voyage (opening 2006)

Indiana Beach, Monticello
Cornball Express
Hoosier Hurricane
Lost Coaster of Superstition Mountain

Iowa

Adventureland, Des Moines
Outlaw
Tornado
Underground

Kentucky

Six Flags Kentucky Kingdom, Louisville
Chang
Greezed Lightnin'
T2
Thunder Run
Twisted Twins (formerly *Twisted Sisters*)

Louisiana

Jazzland, New Orleans
Batman—The Ride
Jester
MegaZeph
Zydeco Scream

Maine

Funtown Splashtown USA, Saco
Excalibur

Maryland

Six Flags America, Largo
Batwing
Joker's Jinx
Mind Eraser
Roar
Superman: Ride of Steel
Two-Face: The Flip Side
Wild One

Massachusetts

Six Flags New England, Agawam
Batman – The Dark Knight
Cyclone
Flashback
Mind Eraser
Mr. Six's Pandemonium
Superman: Ride of Steel
Thunderbolt

Michigan

Michigan's Adventure, Muskegon
Corkscrew
Mad Mouse
Shivering Timbers
Wolverine Wildcat

Minnesota

Valleyfair! Amusement Park, Shakopee
Corkscrew
Excalibur
High Roller
Mad Mouse
Steel Venom
Wild Thing

Missouri

Celebration City, Branson
Ozark Wildcat

Silver Dollar City, Branson
Powder Keg
Thunderation
WildFire

Six Flags St. Louis
Batman—The Ride
The Boss
Mr. Freeze
Ninja
River King Mine Ride
Screamin' Eagle

Worlds of Fun, Kansas City
Boomerang
Mamba
Spinning Dragons
Timber Wolf

Nevada

Buffalo Bill's Resort and Casino, Primm
Stateline Desperado

Circus Circus' Adventuredome,
Las Vegas
Canyon Blaster

New York-New York Hotel and Casino,
Las Vegas
Manhattan Express

Sahara Hotel, Las Vegas
Speed: The Ride

Stratosphere Tower, Las Vegas
Let It Ride High Roller

New Hampshire

Canobie Lake Park, Salem
Canobie Corkscrew
Yankee Cannonball

New Jersey

Clementon Lake Park
Jack Rabbit 2

Morey's Piers, The Wildwoods
Doo Wopper
Great Nor'Easter
Great White
Sea Serpent

Six Flags Great Adventure, Jackson
Batman and Robin: The Chiller
Batman—The Ride
El Toro (opening 2006)
Great American Scream Machine
Kingda Ka
Medusa
Nitro
Rolling Thunder
Runaway Train
Skull Mountain
Superman: Ultimate Flight

New York

Astroland (Coney Island), Brooklyn
Cyclone

The Great Escape, Lake George
Alpine Bobsled
Boomerang
Comet
Nightmare At Crackaxel Canyon
Steamin' Demon

Martin's Fantasy Island, Grand Island
Crazy Mouse
Silver Comet

Playland Park, Rye
Crazy Mouse
Dragon Coaster
Super Flight

Sea Breeze, Rochester
Jack Rabbit

Six Flags Darien Lake, Corfu
Boomerang
Mind Eraser
Predator
Superman: Ride of Steel
Viper

North Carolina

Paramount's Carowinds, Charlotte
BORG Assimilator
Carolina Cyclone
Carolina Gold Rusher
Flying Super Saturator
Hurler
Ricochet
Thunder Road
Top Gun—The Jet Coaster
Vortex

Ohio

Cedar Point, Sandusky
Blue Streak
Cedar Creek Mine Ride
Corkscrew
Disaster Transport
Gemini
Iron Dragon

Magnum XL-200
Mantis
Mean Streak
Millennium Force
Raptor
Top Thrill Dragster
Wicked Twister

Geauga Lake, Aurora
Big Dipper
Dominator
Double Loop
Head Spin
Raging Wolf Bobs
Steel Venom
Thunderhawk
Villain
X-Flight

Paramount's Kings Island, Cincinnati
Adventure Express
The Beast
Face/Off
Flight of Fear
Italian Job: Stunt Track
Racer
Son of Beast
Top Gun
Vortex

Oklahoma

Bell's Amusement Park, Tulsa
Zingo

Frontier City, Oklahoma City
Diamond Back
Silver Bullet
Wildcat

Pennsylvania

Conneaut Lake Park
Blue Streak

Dorney Park, Allentown
Hydra The Revenge
Lazer
Steel Force
Talon
Thunder Hawk
Wild Mouse

Hersheypark, Hershey
Comet
Great Bear
Lightning Racer
Roller Soaker
Sidewinder
SooperDooperLooper
Storm Runner
Trailblazer
Wild Mouse
Wildcat

Kennywood Park, West Mifflin
Exterminator
Jack Rabbit
Phantom's Revenge
Racer
Thunderbolt

Knoebels Amusement Park and Resort, Elysburg
Phoenix
Twister

Lakemont Park, Altoona
Leap The Dips
Skyliner

South Carolina

Family Kingdom, Myrtle Beach
Swamp Fox

Myrtle Beach Pavilion
Hurricane
Mad Mouse

Tennessee

Dollywood, Pigeon Forge
Tennessee Tornado
Thunderhead

Libertyland, Memphis
Revolution
Zippin Pippin

Texas

SeaWorld San Antonio
Great White
Steel Eel

Six Flags Astroworld, Houston
Batman—The Escape
Greezed Lightnin'
Mayan Mindbender
Serial Thriller
Texas Cyclone
Texas Tornado
Ultra Twister
Viper
XLR-8

Six Flags Fiesta Texas, San Antonio
Boomerang
Poltergeist
Rattler
Road Runner Express
Superman Krypton Coaster

Six Flags Over Texas, Dallas
Batman—The Ride
Flashback
Judge Roy Scream
La Vibora
Mr. Freeze
Runaway Mine Train
Runaway Mountain
Shockwave
Texas Giant
Titan

Wonderland, Amarillo
Texas Tornado

Utah

Lagoon, Farmington
Bat
Colossus—Fire Dragon
Roller Coaster

Spider
Wild Mouse

Virginia

Busch Gardens Williamsburg
Alpengeist
Apollo's Chariot
Big Bad Wolf
Loch Ness Monster

Paramount's Kings Dominion, Doswell
Anaconda
Avalanche
Flight of Fear
Grizzly
Hurler
HyperSonic XLC
Italian Job: Stunt Track (opening 2006)
Rebel Yell
Ricochet
Shockwave
Volcano: The Blast Coaster

Washington

Wild Waves and Enchanted Village, Federal Way
Klondike Gold Rusher
Timberhawk: Ride of Prey
Wild Thing

Wisconsin

Mt. Olympus, Wisconsin Dells
Cyclops
Hades
Zeus

International Parks, by country

Australia

Dreamworld, Coomera
Cyclone
Eureka Mountain Mine Ride
Tower of Terror

Warner Bros. Movie World, Oxenford
Lethal Weapon: The Ride
Scooby Doo Spooky Coaster
Superman (opening late 2005)

Wonderland Sydney
Bush Beast
Demon

Austria

Weiner Prater, Vienna
Boomerang
Dizzy-Mouse
Hochschaubahn
Volare
Wild Mouse

Belgium

Bobbejaanland Family Park, Antwerp
Air Race
Bob Express
Looping Star

Revolution
Speedy Bob
Typhoon

Wabili Belgium, Wavre
Calamity Mine
Cobra
Loup-Garou
Tornado
Turbine
Vampire

Brazil

Hopi Hari, Sao Paulo
Katapul
Montezum
Vurang

Terra Encantada, Rio de Janeiro
Monte Makaya

Canada

Calaway Park, Calgary, Alberta
Vortex

Galaxyland Amusement Park, Edmonton, Alberta
Mindbender

Marineland, Niagara Falls, Ontario
Dragon Mountain

Paramount Canada's Wonderland, Vaughan, Ontario
Bat
Dragon Fyre
Fly
Italian Job: Stunt Track
Mighty Canadian Minebuster
Silver Streak
Skyrider
Thunder Run
Tomb Raider: The Ride
Top Gun
Vortex
Wilde Beast

Playland Amusement Park, Vancouver, British Columbia
Corkscrew
Roller Coaster
Wild Mouse

China

Beijing Shijingshan Amusement Park
Atomic Coaster
New Coaster for 2006 TBA

Happy Valley, Shenzhen
Jing Kuan
Shenlin

Hong Kong Disneyland
Space Mountain

Ocean Park, Hong Kong
Dragon
Wild West Mine Train
New Coaster for 2005 TBA

Denmark

Bakken, Klampenborg
Mine Train Ulven
Rutschebanen
New Coaster for 2006 TBA

Fårup Sommerland, Saltum
Falken
Flagermusen

Tivoli Gardens, Copenhagen
Demon
Rutschebanen

England

Alton Towers, Staffordshire
AIR
Black Hole
Corkscrew
Nemesis
Oblivion
Rita—Queen of Speed
Spinball Whizzer

Blackpool Pleasure Beach
Avalanche
Big Dipper
Grand National
Pepsi Max Big One
Revolution
Roller Coaster
Space Invader 2
Steeplechase
Wild Mouse

Chessington World of Adventures,
Surrey
Dragon's Fury
Rattlesnake
Runaway Train
Vampire

Drayton Manor, Staffordshire
G Force
Shockwave

Fantasy Island, Skegness
Fantasy Mouse
Jubilee Odyssey
Millennium Roller Coaster

Flamingo Land, North Yorkshire
Bullet
Corkscrew
Magnum Force
Velocity
Wild Mouse
New Coaster for 2006 TBA

Great Yarmouth Pleasure Beach,
Norfolk
Roller Coaster

Lightwater Valley, North Yorkshire
Rat Ride
Twister
Ultimate

Thorpe Park, Surrey
Colossus
Nemesis Inferno
X:/No Way Out
New Coaster for 2006 TBA

Egypt

Dream Land, Cairo
Dark Coaster
Suspended Coaster

Geroland, Cairo
Boomerang

Magic Land, Cairo
Wild Mouse

Finland

Linnanmäki Park, Helsinki
Tulireki
Vonkaputous
Vuoristorata

Särkänniemi Amusement Park, Tampere
Corkscrew
Halfpipe
Tornado
Trombi

France

Disneyland Resort Paris
Disneyland Park
Big Thunder Mountain Railroad
Indiana Jones and the Temple of Peril
Space Mountain: Mission 2

Walt Disney Studios Park
Rock 'n' Roller Coaster

Parc Astérix, Plailly
Goudurix
Tonerre de Zeux
Trace Du Hourra

Walibi Aquitaine, Roquefort
Boomerang
Zig Zag

Walibi Lorraine, Maizières-les-Metz
Anaconda
Space Comet

Walibi Rhône-Alpes, Les Avenières
Boomerang
Zig Zag

Germany

Europa Park, Rust
Alpenexpress
Atlantica SuperSplash
Euro Mir
Eurosat
Matterhorn-Blitz
Schweizer Bobbahn
Silver Star

Heide Park, Soltau
Big Loop
Colossos
Grottenblitz
Limit
Schweizer Bobbahn

Holiday Park, Hassloch
Expedition GeForce
Super Wirbel

Phantasialand, Bruhl
Colorado Adventure
Temple of the Night Hawk
Winjas
New Coaster for 2006 TBA

Movie Park Germany, Bottrop-
Kirchhellen
Bandit
Cop Car Chase
FX
Mad Manor

Italy

Gardaland, Castelnuovo del Garda
Blue Tornado
Magic Mountain
Sequoia Adventure

Mirabilandia, Savio
Katun
Pakal
Sierra Tonante

Japan

Central Park, Himeji
Diavio

Expoland, Osaka
Daidarasaurus
Fujin Raijin II
Orochi
Space Salamander
Wild Mouse

Fuji-Q Highland, Fujiyoshida-shi
Dodonpa
Fujiyama
Fuwa Fuwa Osora No Dai-Bouken
Mad Mouse

Hakkeijima Sea Paradise, Yokohama
Surf Coaster

Kijima Amusement Park, Beppu City
Gold Stampede
Jupiter
Super LS Coaster

Kobe Portopialand, Hyogo-Ken
BMRX
Double Loop
Munich Autobahn

Nagashima Spa Land, Mei-ken
Corkscrew
Jet Coaster
Looping Star

Steel Dragon 2000
(Currently not operating)
Ultra Twister
White Cyclone
Wild Mouse

Nasu Highland, Nasu
Batflyer
Big Boom
F2 Fright Flight
Panic Drive
Spin Turn
Thunder Coaster

Parque Espana-Shima Spain
Village, Isobe
Gran Montserrat
Pyrenees

Space World, Kita-Kyushu-shi
Black Hole Scramble
Titan
Venus

Summerland, Tokyo
Hayabusa
Tornado

Suzuka Circuitland, Suzuka
Blackout

Tokyo Disneyland
Big Thunder Mountain Railroad
Space Mountain

Tokyo DisneySea
Raging Spirits

Yomiuriland, Tokyo
Bandit
Standing and Loop Coaster
White Canyon

Korea

Everland, Seoul
Eagle Fortress
Rolling X-Train

Lotte World, Seoul
Atlantis Adventure
Comet Express
French Revolution

Mexico

La Feria Chapultepec Magico,
Mexico City
Cascabel
Montaña Rusa
Ratón Loco

Six Flags Mexico, Mexico City
Batman—The Ride
Boomerang
Medusa
Superman el Último Escape

The Netherlands

Efteling, Kaatsheuvel
Bobbaan

Pegasus
Python
Vogel Rok

Toverland, Sevenum
Booster Bike

Walibi World, Biddingshuizen
El Condor
Flying Dutchman Gold Mine
Goliath
Robin Hood
Via Volta
Xpress

Norway

Tusenfryd, Vinterbro
Thundercoaster
Speed Monster (opening 2006)

Spain

PortAventura, Salou
Diablo
Dragon Kahn
Stampida
Tomahawk

Terra Mitica, Benidorm
Magnus Colossus
Tizona

Warner Bros.
Movie World Madrid
Batman La Fuga
Coaster Express
Stunt Fall
Superman: Escape

Sweden

Gröna Lund Amusement Park,
Stockholm
Jetline
Vilda Musen

Liseberg, Göteborg
Balder
Kanonen
Lisebergbanan

Taiwan

Janfusun Fancyworld,
Koo-Kung Hsiang
Crazy Flying Coaster
G5

Vietnam

SaigoMax, Ho Chi Minh City
(under construction)
Dolomite Express
Praire Dog Chase
Rocky Mountain Falls

Wales

Oakwood Leisure Park,
Pembrokeshire
MegaFobia
New Coaster for 2006 TBA

Glossary

Airtime: This all-important term describes the experience of being lifted out of our seats by negative gravitational forces, or "negative Gs." Airtime usually occurs at the tops of hills when our bodies are still moving upward and the coaster's train begins to move downward.

Barrel roll: A very tight inversion that rotates the rider upside-down around, or very near, his center of gravity, as if he were pinwheeling through the inside of a horizontal barrel. Similar to a corkscrew inversion, but with a much smaller radius.

Bobsled coaster: Designed to replicate the sensations of an icy bobsled run, these "trackless" coasters feature roll trains that roll freely through an open trough.

Bunny hops: A row of small hills, usually near the end of a coaster's course, bunny hops are engineered to generate repeated doses of airtime.

Camelback: Simply, this element is a ruler-straight hill or series of hills which, from a distance, looks much like the humps of a camel's back.

Chain lift: This gear-driven metal loop, like a tremendous necklace, is what pulls the traditional coaster up to its highest point, where gravity takes over and the ride begins.

Cobra roll: An inversion element shaped like the hood of a striking cobra, the cobra roll flips and twists riders upside-down twice, sending a train heading in the opposite direction from which it came (i.e., enter a cobra roll heading south and you'll exit heading north). Cobra rolls are found on both standard "sit-down" coasters and inverted coasters.

Continuous-circuit coaster: Roller coasters with a course that is one complete, uninterrupted path are described as a continuous-circuit coasters, which are distinct from shuttle coasters.

Corkscrew: An elongated version of a vertical loop, this inversion element looks very much like a segment from the cork-extracting device from which it gets its name. Corkscrews often come in pairs, though not always.

Diving loop: Found almost exclusively on Bolliger & Mabillard–designed coasters, this inversion both inverts and changes a train's direction, a sort of vertical loop with a perpendicular twist at its peak.

Dueling coaster: Unlike their racing-coaster cousins, double-tracked dueling coasters don't run parallel courses; they create the sensation of near-miss collisions by charging at each other head-on or by nearly sideswiping each other.

Giga-coaster: Any coaster that features a hill or descent of at least 300 feet (91m) in height qualifies.

Heartline camelback: Much like a tight-radius barrel roll, except the upside-down track twirl is at the peak of a hill. See also *Zero-G roll*.

Hypercoaster: Any coaster that features a hill or descent of at least 200 feet (61m) in height qualifies.

Immelman: Taking its name from an acrobatic airplane stunt invented by a German pilot, this is essentially a Bolliger & Mabillard–designed diving loop for an inverted coaster.

Inclined loop: This is used to describe a vertical loop leaned over to the left or right.

Inversion: If it turns you upside-down, it's an inversion.

Inverted coaster: Not to be confused with an inversion, inverted coasters hang fixed-position, non-swinging trains beneath overhead rails. Keep in mind that inverted coasters commonly feature plenty of inversions, though.

Lift hill: If a roller coaster requires some mechanical assistance to gain altitude, it happens on the lift hill, and is ordinarily provided by the chain lift. Nine times out of ten, the first thing riders encounter on a coaster is the lift hill, but there are exceptions. And a number of coasters include several lift hills.

LIM coaster: LIM is the abbreviation for linear induction motor, a high-tech gizmo that propels a coaster train forward on waves of electromagnetic energy. LIM coasters, therefore, do not require lift hills to get up to speed; they are blasted to remarkable velocities by dozens of linear induction motors.

LSM coaster: Similar to LIM coasters, these babies use an even more complicated linear synchronous motor system to handle acceleration chores.

Mine train coaster: Almost always recognizable by their boxy "ore car" vehicles, mine train coasters are comparatively gentle steel coasters, often dressed up with a Wild West theme. Lacking major drops or inversions, these attractions are generally designed for maximum appeal—fun for the whole family, as they say.

Negative Gs: G-forces are the forces of acceleration that affect our bodies while we ride coasters. As the train travels high and low, we feel the sensations of becoming heavier and lighter. For instance, at rest, we experience 1 G, the earth's gravitational pull. But when soaring over a hill, with the train's momentum still pushing up as it begins to head down, we experience less than 1 G, or negative Gs. And that's what produces the weightlessness of airtime.

Out-and-back coaster: Any roller coaster whose course seems to run in one direction, only to have it turn around at the far end and return in a parallel, yet opposite, direction.

Positive Gs: The opposite of negative Gs, positive Gs are what we experience in a roller coaster's valleys, as the train bottoms out and starts to regain altitude. Now, the forces of the train's motion are pushing up towards us and we sink down into the seats, feeling much heavier than normal.

Racing coaster: Fairly self-explanatory, racing coasters feature two or more parallel courses with trains released simultaneously so that they race from start to finish.

Road wheels: Just about every type of roller coaster train sports three sets of wheels to keep it safely and securely on course. The most plainly visible are the road wheels, those that ride on top of the rails. See also *Side-friction wheels* and *Upstop wheels*.

Shuttle coaster: Unlike continuous-circuit coasters, these attractions have two distinct ends. Shuttle coaster trains travel the full length of the course, stop, and then return backwards.

Side-friction wheels: These train wheels are positioned horizontally to roll against either the inside or the outside of a coaster's rails, ensuring that the train cannot derail laterally.

Stand-up coaster: Another easy one—we ride these coasters standing up.

Steel coaster: Regardless of the materials used for its support structure, if a coaster employs steel rails (usually pipe-like tubular steel), it's a steel coaster.

Suspended coaster: Like an inverted coaster, a suspended coaster hangs trains and riders beneath its rail system. However, suspended coaster trains are capable of swinging freely from side to side (which means that, for reasons explained in chapter three, suspended coasters do not include inversions).

Terrain coaster: This describes a roller coaster with hills and valleys that follow the contours of the ground over which it is built.

Twister: Far more complex in layout than an out-and-back coaster, a twister, as its name implies, continuously twists back around into itself, with overlapping layers of track, lots of turns and, ideally, enough changes of direction to completely confuse us.

Upstop wheels: The third set of wheels on a coaster train are the upstop wheels, those that roll against the underside of the rails and keep the train from taking flight as it careens over a pinnacle.

Vertical loop: The most basic form an inversion can take, the vertical loop is a 360-degree track twist standing completely upright. Some are "clothoid" loops (picture an upside-down teardrop shape), while others are more purely circular.

Wild Mouse coaster: These compact steel coasters pretty much share the same design: two-row, four-passenger cars climb to an upper deck where the vehicles zigzag madly back and forth before whistling through several drops and more tight turns.

Wooden coaster: Again, it's all about the rails; wooden coasters are known specifically for their laminated-wood roadbeds, not their supports (though the majority of them do indeed use lumber throughout).

Zero-G roll: An alternative to the term heartline camelback, the Zero-G roll incorporates a near barrel roll at the pinnacle of a hill.

Bibliography

Bennett, David. *Roller Coaster*. Edison: Quintet Publishing Limited, 1998.

Cartmell, Robert. *The Incredible Scream Machine*. Bowling Green: Bowling Green State University Press, 1987.

Kyriazi, Gary. *The Great American Amusement Parks*. Secaucus: Citadel Press, 1976.

Throgmorton, Todd H. *Roller Coasters of America*. Osceola: Motorbooks International Publishers & Wholesalers, 1994.

Urbanowicz, Steven J. *The Roller Coaster Lover's Companion*. Secaucus: Carol Publishing Group, 1997.

Photo Credits

Index

A

Adventure Express (Kings Island), 51
AIR (England's Alton Towers), 89, 141
Airtime, 27, 41
Alcoke, Charles, 17
Allen, John, 22, 25, 27, 43
Alpengeist (Busch Garden Williamsburg), 62, 63, *63*, 64, *64*
American Eagle (Six Flags Great America), 34–35
Amusement parks
  decline of, 13, 20
  fires at, 20
  seaside, 21, *21, 24*, 25
Apollo's Chariot (Busch Garden Williamsburg), 94, 95, *95*
Arrow Development Company, 22
Arrow Dynamics, 51, 54, 59, 61, 91
Avalanche (Wisconsin), 144

B

Bacon, Karl, 61
Baker, Harry, 20
Balder (Sweden), 144
The Bat (Kings Island), 59
Batman & Robin (Six Flags Great America), 74, 76, *76, 77, 77*, 78, *78*, 79, 80
Batman—The Escape (Six Flags AstroWorld), 58
Batman—The Ride (Six Flags Great America), 60, 62, *62*
Batwing (Six Flags America), 89
The Beast (Kings Island), 41, *42*, 43, 44, *44, 45*, 46, 48
Belmont Park (California)
  Giant Dipper, 46, *47*
Ben Hur Chariot Race (Coney Island), 26
Big Bad Wolf (Busch Garden Williamsburg), 59
Bisby's Spiral Airship, 59
BMRX (Japan), 9
Bobs (Coney Island), 9
Bolliger & Mabillard, Inc., 55, 56, 58, 60, 62, 63, 65, 80, 86, 89, 94, 96, 115, 118, 133, 141, 148
Boodley, Michael, 31
The Boss (Six Flags Over St. Louis), 40
Brazil
  Monte Makaya, 54
Busch Gardens Tampa
  Gwazi, 31, 36
  Montu, 62
Busch Gardens Williamsburg
  Alpengeist, 62, 63, *63*, 64, *64*
  Apollo's Chariot, 94, 95, *95*
  Big Bad Wolf, 59
  Loch Ness Monster, 52, 54, *54*

C

California Screamin' (Disney's California Adventure), 48, *49*
Canada
  Le Monstre, 35
  SkyRider, 55
Carowinds (North Carolina)
  Thunder Road, 25
  Vortex, 55, 58, 59, *59*, 60
Cartmell, Robert, 13, 17, 59
Cedar Point
  Gemini, 52, *53*
  Iron Dragon, 60
  Magnum SL-200, 61, 92, *93*
  Mantis, 55, *55*

Millennium Force, 109, *109*, 110, *110*, 111, *111*, 112, 134, 137, 153
Raptor, 60, 62
Wicked Twister, 146
Centrifugal Railways, 15, 16, *16*
Chang (Six Flags Kentucky Kingdom), 55, 57
Church, Frederick, 20, 28, 46
Coasters
  4th Dimension, 146, 147, *147*
  chain lift system, 14
  extreme, 90–131
  first golden age, 20
  floorless, 51, 64–69
  flying, 51, 84–89, 141
  free fall, 115–122
  grooved track, 14–15
  history, 12–23
  impulse, 128–130
  inverted, 22, 51, 60–64
  launched, 51
  linear induction motor, 23, 48, 69–84
  looping, 27, 52–55
  mine, 51–52
  out-and-back, 25–28
  reverse free fall, 122–128
  rocket, 132–139
  second golden age, 25
  shuttle, 51
  side-friction, 17, *18*
  speed racers, 33–39
  stand-up, 23, *50*, 51, 55–58
  steel, 50–89
  suspended, 59–60
  swinging, 51
  terrain, 39–51
  tilting-platform, 136
  twister, 25, 28–31
  wooden, 24–49
Cobra roll, 78, 81, *81*
Collins, Al, 43
Colossus (England's Thorpe Park), 133, 141
Colossus (Six Flags Magic Mountain), *34*, 35, 101, *101*
Coney Island (New York)
  Ben Hur Chariot Race, 26
  Cyclone, 25, 28
  Giant Racer, 26, 28, *28*
  Thunderbolt, 30, *30*
  Tornado, 28, *29*
Construction costs, 8, 44, 59, 65, 69, 86
Corkscrew (Knott's Berry Farm), 52
Corkscrews, 55, 60, 66, 86
Crane, George, 18
Custom Coasters International, 26, 32, 40, 41, 48
Cyclone (Coney Island), 25, 28, 91
Cyclone (Crystal Beach), 20, 28
Cyclone (Six Flags New England), 28

D

Déjà Vu, 88, 136, 148
Desperado, 91
D.H. Morgan Manufacturing Inc., 114
Dinn, Charles, 40, 43
Disney, Walt, 61
Disneyland (California)
  Matterhorn Bobsleds, 20, 22, 51, 61
Disneyland (Hong Kong), 23
Disney's California Adventure
  California Screamin', 48, *49*

Dodonpa (Japan's Fujikyu Highland), 141
Dollywood Park (Tennessee)
  Tennessee Tornado, 61
Dorney Park (Pennsylvania)
  Steel Force, 92, 94, *114*
  Wild Mouse, 142, *142*
Downey, G.W., 59
Dragon Kahn (Spain), 54, 96, *96*
Dueling Dragons (Islands of Adventure), 64

E
Eagle's Fortress (Korea), 60
El Condor (Netherlands), 64
El Toro (Six Flags Great Adventure), 146
England
  AIR, 89, 141
  Grand National, 35
  Nemesis, 64
  Vampire, 60
Excalibur (Valleyfair!), 51
Expedition Everest (Walt Disney World Animal
  Kingdom), 150, *151*

F
Falken (Denmark), 144
Flight of Fear
  Kings Dominion, 71, 73
  Kings Island, 71, 73
Force Engineering, 71
France
  Tonnerre De Zeus, 40
Franco-British Exposition (1908), 18

G
G5 (Taiwan), 118, 148
Gambit (Japan), 64
Gemini (Cedar Point), 52, *53*
Georgia Cyclone (Six Flags Over Georgia), 28
Georgia Scorcher (Six Flags Over Georgia), 56, 58
Germany
  Wild, Wild West, 27
GhostRider (Knott's Berry Farm), *32,* 32–33, *33,*
  40
Giant Dipper (Belmont Park), 46, *47*
Giant Dipper (Santa Cruz Beach Boardwalk), 21,
  21, 24, 25
Giant Racer (Coney Island), 26, 28, *28*
Giga-coasters, 108–115
Giovanola Fréres, 98
Gold Rusher (Six Flags Magic Mountain), 51
Grand National (England), 35
Gravity Group, 40, 152
Gravity Max (Taiwan), 151
Great American Revolution (Six Flags Magic
  Mountain), 52
Great American Scream Machine (Six Flags Over
  Georgia), 25, 27, *27*
Great Coasters International, 30, 31, 36, 48
Great White (Wild Wheels Pier), 25
Greezed Lightnin' (Six Flags AstroWorld), 71
Griffiths, James, 17
Griffiths and Crane Scenic and Gravity
  Railway Company, 18
Grizzly (Kings Dominion), 49, *49*
Gwazi (Busch Gardens Tampa), 31, 36

H
Hades (Wisconsin), 144, *144, 145,* 146
Hain, Clair Jr., 31
Harry C. Baker Company, 28
Hayabusa (Japan), 60
Heartline camelbacks, 66
Heartline spins, 60
Heartline twists, 86
Helix, 46, 48
Hersheypark (Pennsylvania)
  Lightning Racer, 31, 36, 37, *37, 38,* 39
  Wildcat, 31, 36
Hinckle, Philip, 17
Holiday World
  The Legend, 41, *41*
  The Raven, 40, 41
Hoosier Hurricane (Indiana Beach), 25
Hydra: The Revenge (Dorney Park), 96
Hypercoasters, 61, 91–108

I
Ice Slides, 13–14
Impulse coasters, 146
Inclined-Plane Railway, 17
Indiana Beach
  Hoosier Hurricane, 25
Intamin AG, 48, 52, 54, 58, 82, 106, 107, 134,
  144
International Amusement Devices, Inc., 35
International Association of Amusement Parks and
  Attractions, 8
Inversions, 56, 58, 64, 65, 66, 78
  barrel roll, 56, 58, 76
  heartline, 78
  horseshoe, 86
  Immelman, 63
  loop-de-loop, 73
Iron Dragon (Cedar Point), 60
Iron Wolf (Six Flags Great America), 55
Italian Job: Stunt Track (Ohio), 150, *150*
Italy
  Katun, 64

J
J2 (New Jersey), 144
Japan
  Gambit, 64
  Hayabusa, 60
  Mad Cobra, 73, *73*
  Orochi, 64
  Steel Dragon 2000, 8, *90,* 91, 112, *113,* 114
  White Canyon, 27
Jetline (Sweden), 9, *10–11*

K
Kapp, Bruce, 11
Katun (Italy), 64
Keenan, Vernon, 28
Kennywood (Pennsylvania)
  Pippin, 39
  The Racer, 33, 34, *35*
  Thunderbolt, 39, *39*
King Cobra (Kings Island), 55
Kingda Ka (Six Flags Great Adventure),
  138, *139,* 141, 146, *152,* 153
Kings Dominion (Virginia)
  Flight of Fear, 71, 73
  Grizzly, 49, *49*
  Rebel Yell, 25, 35

Shockwave, 55
Kings Island (Ohio)
  Adventure Express, 51
  The Bat, 59
  The Beast, 41, *42,* 43, 44, *44, 45,* 46, 48
  Flight of Fear, 71, 73
  King Cobra, 55
  The Racer, 22, 23, 25
  Son of Beast, 27, 101, 102, *103,* 104, *104,*
    105, *105,* 108
  Top Gun, 60
  Volcano, 80, 82, *82,* 83, *83,* 84
Knott's Berry Farm (California)
  Corkscrew, 52
  GhostRider, 32, 32–33, *33,* 40
  Montezooma's Revenge, 70, 71, *71*
  Xcelerator, 136, *136*
Knudsen, R., 17
Korea
  Eagle's Fortress, 60
Kraken (SeaWorld Orlando), 69

L
La Marcus Thompson Switchback Railway (Coney
  Island), 16
Larrick, Denise, 40
Leap The Dips (Lakemont Park), 17
The Legend (Holiday World), 41, *41*
Le Monstre (Canada), 35
Les Montagnes Russes à Belleville (France), 15,
  15
Lightning Racer (Hersheypark), 31, 36, 37, *37,*
  38, 39
Loch Ness Monster (Busch Garden Williamsburg),
  52, 54, *54*
Looff, Arthur, 20, 25
Loops, 52–55
  dive, 55, 56, 58, 66
  inclined, 55
  shuttle, 70
  vertical, 48, 56, 58, 60, 66, 86, 96, 102

M
Mad Cobra (Japan), 73, *73*
Magnum XL-200 (Cedar Point), 61, 91, 92, *93*
Mantis (Cedar Point), 55, *55*
Matterhorn Bobsleds (Disneyland), 20, 22, 51, 61
Mauch Chunk Switchback Railroad, 16
Mechanical Electric Race Course (France), 15
Megaphobia (Wales), 40
Mexico
  Serpiente De Fuego, 35
Michigan's Adventure
  Shivering Timbers, 26, 27, 40
Millennium Force (Cedar Point), 109, *109,* 110,
  110, 111, *111,* 112, 133, 134
Miller, John, 17, 18, 20, 33, 39
Mind Bender (Six Flags Over Georgia), 54
Mind Eraser (Six Flags Elitch Gardens), 89, *89*
Mr. Freeze (Six Flags Over St. Louis), 73, 80, *81*
Monte Makaya (Brazil), 54
Montezooma's Revenge (Knott's Berry Farm), 70,
  71, *71*
Montu (Busch Gardens Tampa), 62
Morgan, Ed, 61
Motorbike Launch Coaster, 148, 149

N
Nemesis (England), 64
Netherlands
  El Condor, 64
Nickell, Jim, 43
Ninja (Six Flags Magic Mountain), 60, *60*

O
Oblivion (England), 115, *115,* 116, *116,* 117,
  118, 141, 148
Orient Express (World of Fun), 54
Orochi (Japan), 64
Ozark Wildcat (Missouri), 144

P
Palisade Amusement Park (New Jersey), 23, *23*
Paramount Parks, 22
Pearce, Fred, 20
Pepsi Max Big One (England), 91
Philadelphia Toboggan Company, 18, 22, 26, 43
Pippin (Kennywood), 39
Poltergeist (Six Flags Fiesta Texas), 72, *72,* 73
Premier Rides, 71, 72, 73, 74
Price, William, 41
Prior, Frank, 20, 28, 46
Promenades Aeriennes (France), 14, *14,* 15
Psyclone (Six Flags Magic Mountain), 28

R
The Racer (Kennywood), 33, 34, *35*
The Racer (Kings Island), 22, 23, 25
Raging Bull (Six Flags Great America), 94, *94*
Rampage (Visionland), 40
Raptor (Cedar Point), 60, 62
Rattler (Six Flags Fiesta Texas), 27
The Raven (Holiday World), 40, 41
Rebel Yell (Kings Dominion), 25, 35
Reed, William, 43
Revenge of the Mummy (Universal Studios), 150
Riddler's Revenge (Six Flags Magic Mountain), *50,*
  51, 56, *56,* 57, *57,* 58
Roadrunner Express (Six Flags Fiesta Texas), 51
Roar! (Six Flags America), 31
Roar! (Six Flags Marine World), 30, 31
Rocket coasters, 132–139
Roller Coaster Corporation of America, 27, 48
Rolling Thunder (Six Flags Great Adventure), 146
Runaway Mine Train (Six Flags Fiesta Texas), 51
Russian Mountains, 14, 16

S
Safety, 8, 15
Santa Cruz Beach Boardwalk
  Giant Dipper, 21, 21, 24, 25
Scenic Railway (Atlantic City), 17
Schwarzkopf, Anton, 52, 54, 70, 71
Schwarzkopf/Zierer, 9
Screamin' Eagle (Six Flags Over St. Louis), 25–26
Screaming Squirrel, 142
Sequoia Adventure (Italy), 143, *143*
Serpiente De Fuego (Mexico), 35
SheiKra (Busch Gardens), 96, 118, 148, 149, *149*
Shivering Timbers (Michigan's Adventure), 26,
  27, 40
Shockwave (Kings Dominion), 55
Shock Wave (Six Flags Over Texas), 54
Silver Star (Europa Park), 96
Six Flags America
  Roar!, 31

Six Flags AstroWorld
  Batman—The Escape, 58
  Greezed Lightnin,' 71
  Texas Cyclone, 28
Six Flags Fiesta Texas
  Mr. Freeze, 73, 74, *75*, 80, *81*
  Poltergeist, 72, *72*, 73
  Rattler, 27
  Roadrunner Express, 51
  Runaway Mine Train, 51
  Superman Krypton Coaster, 69
  Texas Giant, 30
Six Flags Great Adventure
  Medusa, 65, *65*, 66, *67*, *68*, 69
Six Flags Great America
  American Eagle, 34–35
  Batman & Robin, 74, 76, *76*, 77, *77*, 78, *78*,
    79, 80
  Batman—The Ride, 60, 62, *62*
  Iron Wolf, 55
  Nitro, 94, 95, 97, *97*, 98
  Raging Bull, 94, *94*
  Viper, 28
Six Flags Kentucky Kingdom
  Chang, 55, 57
  Twisted Sisters, 35, 36, *36*, 40
Six Flags Magic Mountain
  Colossus, *34*, 35, 101, *101*
  Gold Rusher, 51
  Goliath, 98, *99*, 100, *100*, 101
  Great American Revolution, 52
  Ninja, 60, *60*
  Psyclone, 28
  Riddler's Revenge, *50*, 51, 56, *56*, 57, *57*, 58
  Superman: The Escape, *122*, 123, *123*, 124,
    124, 125, 127
  X, 146, 147, *147*
Six Flags Marine World
  Roar!, 30, 31
Six Flags New England
  Cyclone, 28
Six Flags of Adventure
  The Villain, 40
Six Flags Over Georgia
  Georgia Cyclone, 28
  Georgia Scorcher, 56, 58
  Great American Scream Machine, 25, 27, *27*
  Mind Bender, 54
Six Flags Over St. Louis
  The Boss, 40
  Mr. Freeze, 73, 80, *81*
  Screamin' Eagle, 25–26
Six Flags Over Texas
  Shock Wave, 54
Sky Princess (Dutch Wonderland), 40
Sky Rider (Canada), 55
Son of Beast (Kings Island), 27, 101, 102, *103*,
  104, *104*, 105, *105*, 108, 146
Spain
  Dragon Kahn, 54, 96, *96*
  Stampida, 35
Spirals, 58, 63, 66, 86, 92
Spires, 70
S&S Power Inc., 61, 118–123, 134
Stampida (Spain), 35
Stealth (Great America), 85, *85*, 86, *87*, 88, 89
Steel Dragon 2000 (Japan), 8, *90*, 91, 112, *113*,
  114
Steel Phantom (Kennywood), 91

Steel Venom (Geauga Lake), 128, 129
Steel Venom (Minnesota), 146
Steeplechase Ride (Coney Island), 17, *18*
Stengel Engineering, 137
Storm Runner (Hersheypark), 135, 136, *136*, 137
Stratosphere (Las Vegas), 130
Summers, Curtis D., 30
Superman: The Escape, 8, 106, *122*, 123, *123*
Superman Krypton Coaster (Six Flags Fiesta Texas), 69
Superman: Ultimate Flight (Six Flags Great Adventure),
  96
Superman: Ultimate Flight (Six Flags Over Georgia),
  89, *132*, 133, 134, *140*, 142

T
Tennessee Tornado (Dollywood Park), 61
Texas Cyclone (Six Flags AstroWorld), 28
Texas Giant (Six Flags Fiesta Texas), 30
Thompson, La Marcus, 15, 16, 17, 18
Thrust Air 2000, 118–123
ThuNderaTion (Silver Dollar City), 51
Thunderbolt (Coney Island), 30, *30*
Thunderbolt (Kennywood), 39, *39*
Thunderhead (Dollywood), 143, 144
Thunder Road (Carowinds), 25
Tilyou, George, 17
Timberhawk: Ride of Prey (Washington), 144
Togo, 55, 130
Tonnerre De Zeus (France), 40
Top Gun (Kings Island), 60
Top Thrill Dragster (Cedar Point), 134, *134*, 141
Tornado (Coney Island), 9, *9*, 28, *29*
Tower of Terror (Australia), 127–128
Traver, Harry, 20, 26
Trick-track, 26
Twisted Twins (Six Flags Kentucky Kingdom), 35, 36,
  36, 40

V
V2 (Six Flags Marine World), 146
Vampire (England), 60
Velocity (England), 149
Vekoma Rides Manufacturing, 64, 80, 84, 88, 89,
  141
Vettel, Andy, 39
The Villain (Six Flags of Adventure), 40
Viper (Six Flags Great America), 28
Volcano (Kings Island), 80, 82, *82*, 83, *83*, 84
Vortex (Carowinds), 55, 58, 59, *59*, 60
Voyage (Indiana), 146, 152

W
Wales
  MegaFobia, 40
Weightlessness, 60, 63
White Canyon (Japan), 27
Wicked Twister (Cedar Point), 146
Wild Mouse (Dorney Park), *142*
Wild, Wild West (Germany), 27
Wildcat (Hersheypark), 31, 36
Wild Wheels Pier (New Jersey)
  Great White, 25

X
X (Six Flags Magic Mountain), 61, 146, *147*
Xcelerator (Knott's Berry Farm), *132*, 133, 136
X-Flight (Geauga Lake), 89